TRANSITIONS

Fiction, Poetry, and Non-Fiction

DOUGLAS HILKER

BARRY DUNCAN

SUE HARPER

ANDREA MOZAROWSKI

HARCOURT
BRACE
CANADA

HARCOURT BRACE & COMPANY, CANADA

TORONTO·ORLANDO·SAN DIEGO·LONDON·SYDNEY

Canadian Cataloguing in Publication Data
Main entry under title:
Transitions: fiction, poetry, and non-fiction

ISBN 0-7747-0151-X

1. Readers (Secondary).   2. Language arts (Secondary).
I. Hilker, Douglas.

PE 1121.T73   1994   808'.0427   C94-931816-7

Douglas Hilker: Head of English, Runnymede Collegiate Institute, City of York Board of Education
Barry Duncan: Head of the English and Media Arts Department, School of Experiential Education, Etobicoke Board of Education
Sue Harper: Head of English, John Fraser Secondary School, Peel Board of Education
Andrea Mozarowski: English Teacher, Upper Canada College

Editorial Director: *Hans Mills*
Acquisitions Editor: *Maggie Goh*
Senior Editor: *Lydia Fletcher*
Project Editor: *Robin Rivers*
Senior Production Editor: *Elizabeth Salomons*
Senior Art Director: *Arnold Winterhoff*
Computer Layout and Design: *Anita Macklin*
Junior Designer: *Cathy MacLean*
Permissions Editor: *Sarah Byck*
Photo Research: *Liz Kirk*
Cover Illustration: *Kevin N. Ghiglione*

∞ Printed in Canada on acid-free paper

3 4 5   03 02 01 00 99

Acknowledgements

The authors and publisher gratefully acknowledge these reviewers for their contribution to the development of this project:

Elizabeth Fraser—English Department Head, Grande Prairie Composite High School, Grande Prairie, Alberta

Dawn Marshall—English Teacher, Dartmouth High School, Dartmouth, Nova Scotia

Allan McPherson—English Department Head, Regina Mundi College, London, Ontario

Ian Mills—English Department Head, Lester B. Pearson High School, Burlington, Ontario

Barbara Mitchell—English Teacher, Rosedale Heights Secondary School, Toronto, Ontario

Steve Naylor—English Teacher, Salmon Arm Senior Secondary School, Salmon Arm, British Columbia

Richard Neff—English Teacher/Teacher Librarian, Centre Wellington District High School, Fergus, Ontario

Carol Richards—English Teacher, Scarlett Heights Collegiate, Etobicoke, Ontario

Lisa Spano—English Teacher, Loyalist Collegiate and Vocational Institute, Kingston, Ontario

Barbara Terpstra—English Department Head, Jarvis Collegiate, Toronto, Ontario

Zubeda Vahed—Multiculturalism Race Relations Officer, Peel Board of Education, Mississauga, Ontario

Table of Contents

Be Yourself

Out of the House

On the Streets

Fitting In

Natural Environments

Expressing Yourself in a High-Tech World

Connecting With Nature

Living With Nature

Learning From Nature

The Impact of Technology

Living With Technology

Applying Technology

The Arts in Action

To the Reader

Transitions invites you to think more deeply about the personal concerns and global issues that affect your life. Responding to our changing world requires all of us to think about people and events in new ways. It is important to listen to the many voices of our society, including those of men, women, and children of the many cultures represented in our country. Once we do this, we can make intelligent choices about working and living together for the benefit of all.

Reading the selections and working through the activities in this text will help you gain insights, and develop the critical thinking and language skills that will help you be successful not only in English class, but in all subjects areas. The skills you are developing now will help you get a job, get accepted into post-secondary educational institutions, and be successful at whatever you choose to do.

Transitions is divided into three **units**. The first unit, "You and Others," raises questions about identity. Your family, friends, cultural background, and gender influence the way you see yourself and relate to society. The second unit, "Your Environments," focusses on your habitat. The time you spend at the mall, on the streets, in your neighbourhood, and relating to nature affects the quality of your life in many ways. The third unit, "Expressing Yourself in a High-Tech World," explores the role of the arts and technology in your life. They can enrich you and help you to use your knowledge, skills, and values to make a contribution to society.

The **Activities** have been designed to help you interpret and appreciate the selections, and to give you and your classmates the opportunity to explore the ideas in them in a variety of enjoyable and educational ways. Some of the activities encourage you to integrate your knowledge from other subjects and make connections based on your personal interests. **Content and Style Activities** are designed to support your understanding of what the selection is about and how it is presented. **Social Context Activities** intend to promote your understanding of the powerful influence that personal relationships, media, and society have on your life. **Personal and Imaginative Response Activities** relate to the themes and issues in the selections. The **Unit Activities** provide an opportunity for you to do further research on topics explored in the unit and undertake projects such as creating anthologies and making presentations to the class.

Power Tools (pages 75–89) provide you with tips on how to complete some of the more complex activities such as making a video or participating in a debate. A glossary of terms used in the text is also included.

Evaluation

It is important for you to understand what learning outcomes you will be expected to demonstrate during the year. The activities in this text will help you practise, develop, and demonstrate a wide variety of language skills. These skills can be acquired through working in a large group, a small group, or independently. Some of these skills are listed below. Ask your teacher for a more complete list of the learning outcomes that you will be evaluated on this year.

Information Gathering: reading, talking and listening, researching, note-taking, accessing media and technology

Information Processing: critical thinking, questioning, idea gathering and discussing, writing listing/charting/outlining, adapting/rewriting/recasting/re-creating

Information Sharing: writing and speaking in a variety of formats for a variety of purposes and audiences, following correct conventions of language, making presentations, creating visual representations, using technology (video/audio taping, word processing), dramatizing, completing assignments, tests, and exams

Tracking Your Progress

Evaluation is important. Your teacher's evaluation will give you important information on how well you are doing. However, your own **self-evaluation** will help you track the progress you have made towards meeting both expected standards and personal goals.

One excellent way of tracking your progress is to keep a **learning log**. Once a week or at the end of each set of activities that you complete, answer some of the following questions in your log:

1) What do I know now that I didn't know before?
2) What evidence can I give to show that I have become a better reader, viewer, writer, speaker, listener, researcher, and/or group member?
3) What have I found out about the way I learn best (i.e., independently, in groups, at school, at home)?
4) How have I integrated non-print media in my learning (such as accessing television, using a tape recorder or video camera, etc.)?

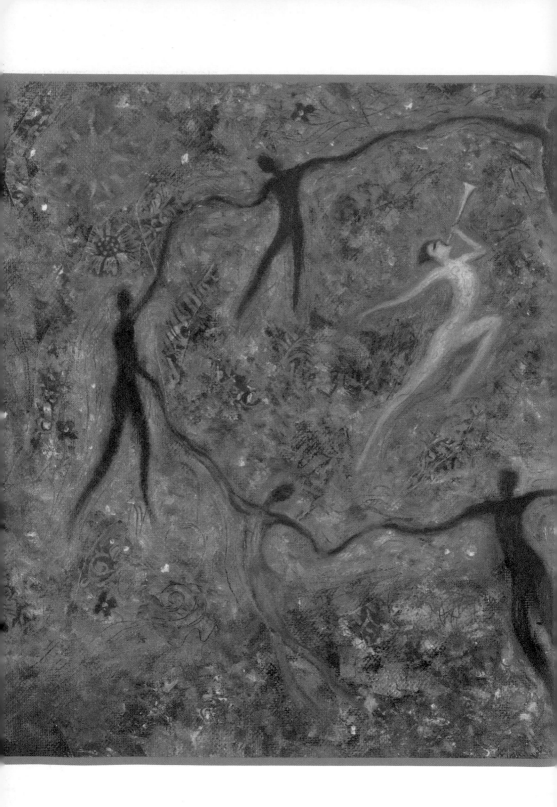

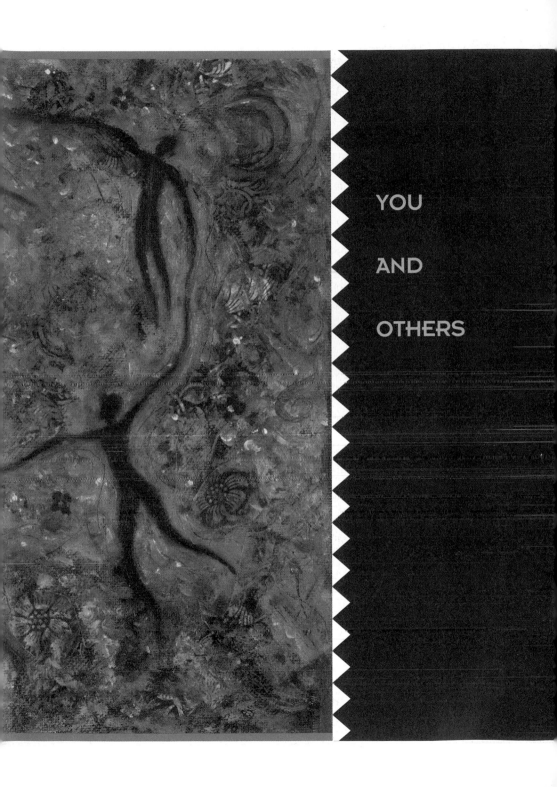

YOU

AND

OTHERS

Oranges

BY GARY SOTO

[handwritten: ↓ the snail 🐌]

The first time I walked
With a girl, I was twelve, *[handwritten: déprimer du fait qu'il a 2 orange dans sa poche]*
Cold, and <u>weighted down</u>
With two oranges in my jacket.
December. Frost cracking
Beneath my steps, my breath
Before me, then gone,
As I walked toward
Her house, the one whose
<u>Porch</u> light burned yellow *[handwritten: balcon]* *[handwritten: the light is alway up.]*
Night and day, in any weather.
A dog <u>barked</u> at me, until *[handwritten: japper]*
She came out pulling
At her gloves, face bright
With <u>rouge</u>. I smiled, *[handwritten: 1. joue rouge 2. make up.]*
Touched her shoulder, and led
Her down the street, across
A used car lot and a line
Of newly planted trees,
Until we were breathing
Before a <u>drugstore</u>. We *[handwritten: pharmacie]*
Entered, the tiny bell
Bringing a saleslady
Down a <u>narrow aisle</u> of goods. *[handwritten: petite rangé]*
I turned to the candies *[handwritten: Similes étage]*
<u>Tiered like bleachers</u>, *[handwritten: board ranger par étage]*
And asked what she wanted—
<u>Light in her eyes, a smile</u> *[handwritten: métaphore]*
Starting at the corners
Of her mouth. I fingered

2

A nickel in my pocket,
And when she lifted a chocolate
That cost a dime,
I didn't say anything.
I took the nickel from
My pocket, then an orange,
And set them quietly on
The counter. When I looked up,
The lady's eyes met mine,
And held them, knowing
Very well what it was all
About.

       Outside,
A few cars hissing past,
Fog hanging like old
Coats between the trees.
I took my girl's hand
In mine for two blocks,
Then released it to let
Her unwrap the chocolate.
I peeled my orange
That was so bright against
The gray of December
That, from some distance,
Someone might have thought
I was making a fire in my hands.

[Handwritten annotations:]
5¢

he need more monnie.

I don't have monné but I want to pay with a nickel and an orange

Ele a comprit.
(marchande)

Brouillard

Similes (like or as)

débaler

éplucher

metaphore.

brightness = Shine

metaphor: the orange is being compared to a fire.

3

■ Content and Style

1. In a few sentences, write the story the poem tells.

2. Describe the events of the poem from the girl's point of view.

3. With a partner, choose one sentence in the poem that could apply to most first dates. Choose another sentence that contains specific details about the first date in this poem. Compare your choices with those made by another pair of students.

4. a) Find two things that are being compared to something else in the last six lines of the poem. Use the glossary (page 86) to decide whether each comparison is a simile or a metaphor.

   b) Write your own example of a simile and a metaphor and label them.

■ Social Context

5. With a partner, role play a conversation between the woman in the store and a friend when she discusses what happened in the store.

6. With a partner of the opposite sex, reread the poem and make the following two lists:

   a) phrases from the poem that suggest the boy and girl have a positive relationship

   b) phrases that suggest the relationship might run into trouble

   Present your lists to the class.

■ Personal and Imaginative Response

7. Use the poem as a model to write your own poem about a young man or woman's first date. Include a simile or a metaphor or both.

8. Write about your own first date or the first time you really liked someone.

I Loved My Friend

BY LANGSTON HUGHES

I loved my friend.
He went away from me.
There's nothing more to say.
The poem ends,
Soft as it began— Simile
I loved my friend.

■ Content and Style

1. Explain why the following three words are important to the poem: "loved," "nothing," and "soft." Write one sentence about the importance of each word.

2. Choose three words that describe the mood of the narrator. Explain to a partner why you chose each one.

■ Social Context

3. a) List qualities you think a good friend should have.
   b) With a partner, decide whether a member of the same sex or the opposite sex makes a better friend.
   c) Find out how other people in the class responded to (b).

■ Personal and Imaginative Response

4. With a partner, role play what might have happened the last time that the two friends in the poem saw each other.

5. Write a letter the lost friend might send to the narrator after reading the poem.

6. Bring to class a song that says something important about friendship. Play it for your classmates and explain why you chose it.

7. Create a poem, song, or drawing to express your feelings about one of your best friends.

Dave's Fall

BY ANDREA HOLTSLANDER

In fall I see stained glass sky *tache*
and (elm trees like arches) *similes*
in an abandoned cathedral.
   Dave says he hears orange sound.
I can only imagine,
Maybe it's (the sound of an absent wind) *métaphor*
no longer brushing against fallen leaves
that lie crisp in (dusty sunlight,) *métaphor*
   but he can't see the sunlight,
only hears orange sound
as his white cane
sweeps through the leaves.

grand geste

Activities DAVE'S FALL

■ Content and Style

1. a) Find words or groups of words in the poem that you have
      trouble understanding. With a partner, decide what you
      think the words mean and why the poet might have used
      them.

   b) Discuss with the class any words you still have trouble
      understanding.

2. a) Write the words from the first three lines of the poem that create the picture or image of fall being like a cathedral.
   b) Reread the poem to find images that include colour.
   c) Decide how these images add to the meaning of the poem. Share your ideas with classmates.

■ Social Context

3. a) Have a classmate blindfold you and guide you in a walk around the classroom or hallway. Pay special attention to what you hear, touch, and smell.
   b) When your walk is complete, write a paragraph describing your experience. What sounds, smells, and physical sensations do you remember? What did it feel like to be cut off from your sense of sight?

4. a) In a small group, list ways in which your community is making it easier for people who are disabled to take part in society.
   b) Compare your list with those of other groups.
   c) On your own, explain in a paragraph whether or not the government should pay for the cost of these changes.

5. Interview a person with a disability in your school or community. Find out
   a) what buildings or places the person has difficulty entering and exiting, and
   b) which entrances could be improved.

■ Personal and Imaginative Response

6. Write a poem or paragraph about a friend or relative who is disabled.

7. Copy "Dave's Fall" on a sheet of paper and create artwork or a collage to illustrate it.

8. Rewrite the poem from Dave's point of view and give the new poem a title.

Dying for Love

BY MARTHA BROOKS

I'm in love with Philip Chester. Oh, why couldn't I have been born a blonde? I have hair that looks like it's been soaked overnight in a coffee pot. And mud-green eyes. And, God how I hate them, freckles. I've tried Porcelana on these freckles. I've lain for hours with lemon slices on my face. I've delicately applied Revlon's Touch and Glow and worked over each of God's little sun-kisses with generous smears of cover-up stick, but nothing works.

I could bleach my hair but my mother won't let me until I'm an old maid. I'm saving up to buy some pearly sea-foam eyeshadow. I don't mind being tall or that my shoulders are broad; I look great in sweaters. But the freckles are hopeless. They were cute when I was six. What do I do now that I'm fourteen?

Philip Chester, whom I have loved from afar since I was in grade three and he was in grade five (I'm mad for his kisses and he's kissed more girls than a dog in June drops grey ticks), likes girls who are tiny-faced baby dolls.

Yesterday, I had no intention of sending the note I wrote in science class. Marti Panchuk found it in the hall where it had dropped out of my notebook, and she *pinned it up on the school bulletin board* for everyone to see. Including Philip! Oh God, I wanted to die. If it had just been an ordinary love note. But oh no! Miss Blabbermouth of the Century had to tell him how much she'd like to get him alone and cover him with kisses, because he's so sweet—like a giant candy cane. We are talking megamortification here.

If I'd been Lucia di Lammermoor or Tosca or Madama Butterfly I could have fallen down, shrieking and stabbing myself, and that would have ended it. The tragedy of real life is that the prime causes of personal anguish are often hilarious to lookers-on. At the opera? All the world's great love themes get played out properly and people die horribly, slowly, and for the right reasons. Nobody

9

laughs. There isn't a single real-life person anymore who's willing to die for love.

My mother's going through early menopause and I'm going through late puberty. She doesn't have freckles or wrinkles. I found her on her hands and knees on the floor when I came home from school. I was skipping last class because I could no longer tolerate my snickering classmates or the whole rest of Sandler Collegiate, where I am a low-life junior, as if that weren't in itself enough to cause me to jump off a bridge.

With a wet blue J-cloth and a broken fingernail, she flicked away splatters of dried-up fudge brownie batter from the kitchen floor tiles. "I wish you would be neater in the kitchen," she sighed one of her sighs, then looked up as I stood there needing her to say something a little more relevant about my life. I screamed at her. I swore at her. A blanked-out expression, and then a hot flush as she screwed up her pretty-as-a-flower face. She stood. "Ardis!" she screamed. "Go up to your room!"

"My pleasure," I said, and turned and went upstairs. I slammed into my room and dove, in tears, onto my navy-and-peach patch-work quilt. My fat old tabby cat bounced into the air from a sound sleep and squawked like a sat-on squeeze-toy as his feet hit the floor.

I have never in my life sworn at my mother. I've just thought about it lots of times. She thinks she owns me. She doesn't like anything I like (except the opera). She yells at me for the slightest little thing. She nags. She lectures. She wants me to be perfect like she isn't.

Every other mother I know works at an important job. It's embarrassing to tell kids that my mother is a cheer lady every Thursday afternoon at the hospital, pushing around carts of pep-permints and year-old magazines. She also volunteers Tuesdays on Palliative Care, where they put all the patients who are dying. Her favourite colour used to be peach. We even had a peach sofa and matching love seat. Now that she plays Florence Nightingale, she's passionate about leaf green. Says it's an Alive Colour. I won't let her touch my room. I hate green.

In the halls today, first thing as the hot morning sun shooed us off the street to scurry like rats to our classes, Lisa Malone caught up with me. Her quite small blue eyes sparkled maliciously. This is the third time she's talked to me this year. "God, I can't believe you

wrote that to him," she burbled. "I wouldn'ta had the guts to do it. Whattid he say, anyways? I mean, he musta flipped." She blew a pink bubble and snapped it, backwards, into her gloss-sticky mouth.

"Lisa, your hair looks like something my cat regurgitated," I said, pushing past her for math class. Lisa, who has perfect hair (she keeps hair spray, mousse, gel, and a curling iron in her locker) looked stricken, then said, "Geez, Ardis. You don't have to take a major. Like, it isn't the end of your life or anything."

Then a miracle happened. Marti passed me a note in math class. It said: "Don't feel bad. Phil really likes you. No kidding. Sorry about yesterday. Write back if we're still friends."

I've never been friends with Marti. Nobody's friends with Marti. She lives in the constant glow of romance (not her own, everyone else's). To be friends with her is to admit you're a total social washout. But I had to risk it so I could ask, "How do you know Phil really likes me?"

"Because he told me," said Marti, turning around, pushing her fishy glasses back on her nose, blinking her bulgy carp eyes.

Phil is sixteen and the tallest boy in school. He hangs around with Bobby Ferreira and Gordon Field, who date the same type of girls as he does: blonde and perfect like Lisa. If Phil stands over you, when you can get close enough for that, the world falls away and you can't breathe. Not that you need to, much. What's so great about breathing anyway? The purest most beautiful notes in opera are surrounded by the rarified air of love and anguish, and I can hold my breath as long as any opera star alive. I've done it, sitting in the darkened concert hall, pierced to the heart while a note goes on and on and everyone else in the audience breathes and coughs.

The buzzer goes. I find my feet as Marti disappears in a crowd of heads, before I can get the chance to ask the whens and whats of Philip Chester liking me. She's keeping me hanging so I'll have to talk to her again. I'm jostled into the hallways, carried along by a stream of kids. Some leave the stream, swallowed up by their appointed classrooms; others flow into the stream. There is, as well, a stream coming from the other direction. I have to pass through that one, as do several people ahead of me. The streams converge in confusion. I struggle to the other side. Philip Chester is coming out of Science Lab. It must be an omen! People push past us. He takes my arm and gently steers me off to one side. I am dizzy. I may possibly faint. The top of my head comes as far as his open shirt collar. He smiles shyly and deliciously. His eyes are smoky blue. His dark brown hair falls over his forehead. I should be dying of embarrassment but instead I'm dying for love. He must be the sweetest boy in the universe. I don't know if I can hold my breath much longer.

Then, quietly breaking the spell and my heart, he says, "It was pretty funny what you wrote yesterday. Too bad you signed it. Marti will believe anything. I really blew up at her. It was a joke, eh Ardis?"

He doesn't mean to be cruel. He just is. He can't stand it, what I wrote about him. He wants me to tell him, out loud, the six years of this feeling that has grown up inside me has been a lie.

At the kitchen table, Mom's scrunched over paper and figures. She keeps the accounts for Dad's printing business. I flop down into the chair across the table from her, books still in my arms. Without looking up from adding a column of figures, she says, "I'm making your favourite kind of chicken for supper. Do you want noodles or brown rice?"

"Doesn't matter," I shrug.

She looks up then, takes off her glasses, props them on her head. Parental radar scans my face for clues. "How's school?"

"All right," I push back on my chair. Lightly kick the table leg.

She watches me steadily. I don't tell her stuff. She used to try to drag it out of me. All I want is a hug. She wants a discussion.

She says, "I'm going over to Palliative Care tonight. Visiting someone who'd really cheer you up. Want to come?"

Doesn't matter.

On the way over to the hospital Mom is real quiet. She's trying to quit smoking. This is the fourth time she's tried. Our car smells fresher these past two weeks and the ashtray overflows with gum wrappers. With one hand she manoeuvers the steering wheel as the tires lick up the dark streets. Purse between her knees, she fumbles for gum and comes up with two squares of Fleer's Double-Bubble. "Want one?" she says, holding it out.

"Reverting, are we? Going through our second childhood?" I say, making an effort at gaiety so she won't keep stealing anxious looks at me. It works. She chuckles. When she's not in a state of menopausal hysteria, we can sometimes joke around.

I unwrap the gum and watch graceful black lampposts slip by. They're all along the river near the hospital, and are softened by imitation gaslights. They call this section of the street The Promenade, and the rich orangey lights and people casually sauntering along the riverside and near the old stone Roman Catholic cathedral make you feel as if you're caught in a time warp.

The hospital is run by nuns. There are crosses everywhere and God Loves You plaques. Religious fervour gives me the creeps. It's ten to nine, past the usual visiting hours. A security officer who's been sitting near the elevators, looking at his shoes, gets up and tells Mom she's not going any further unless she gets a pass. She produces a little red card, grandly flashes it at him. As if it were orchestrated, he backs off and at the same time some elevator doors open. We step inside. We're the only passengers. Mom leans back, folds her arms across her ultra-suede trench coat, looks sidelong at me, and blows a bubble that immediately bursts.

The doors to all the rooms are posted with elongated signs in black vertical oriental lettering. "They say Welcome in Chinese," Mom explains. "One of the nurses is taking a course in calligraphy."

Beside the Chinese welcome on 528 is a small hanging basket of silk irises and tulips. The doors to most of the rooms are open. This one is partly closed. Mom raps lightly before hesitantly entering the room. It's occupied by two patients. A nurse in a white pantsuit and belted cardigan sweater pulls across a curtain between the beds. She adjusts the IV on the youngish woman who is closest to us and smiles distantly in our direction before she leaves the room. The dark-haired woman lies on her back. In a chair that is pulled right up beside her is a man. Like her, he is probably in his late twenties. His hair is too short, like he's just got it cut. We see him from the back; his ears are red, his head droops. Her hand on the bedspread almost touches his. She talks softly, though her eyes are closed.

Standing near the window, arms folded, looking out, is the patient I presume we've come to see. She turns, smiles when she sees it's us. She's tanned. An Arizona retiree-type grandmother with steel grey hair who looks too healthy to be dying. She wears a flowing mint-green satin gown over the standard nondescript blue that's always too short even if you're a midget.

We come together and whisper for a while, like three worn-out geese in a deaf-making wind. The woman is a smiler. Even her eyes smile. I feel as if I've known her all my life. With both hands she touches my shoulders and tells my mother I'm a beauty. Her name is Rachel.

With a kind of cautious grace she inches over to her bed, sits on the edge. "I'm going home tomorrow, Ida," she says, and softly enfolds her bare feet under the covers. "Just for a few days. My son and my two grandchildren are coming to collect me."

I get this mental picture of bits of Rachel spread all over the room. The children pasting her together, giggling over which pieces fit where. Setting her on a chaise longue. Decorating her hair with purple irises and orange tulips.

"Rachel is an opera star," says my mother, out of the blue. She nods and smiles at me, then at Rachel who smiles brilliantly back.

"Used to be," corrects Rachel. "That was a long time ago. I still love my music." She plays with a heavy gold ring, set with an enormous dark-coloured gem, on the fourth finger of her right hand. "Your mother tells me you two never miss the opera."

The young man abruptly appears from behind the curtain separating Rachel and her neighbour. "I'm stepping out. Going for a coffee," he interjects.

Rachel immediately lifts her head to him. "I'll listen for her," she says.

He runs one hand over his inch-long hair, shoves the other hand into his pocket, and without another word disappears.

Rachel smooths and folds the edge of her sheet. "Poor things," she says gently. "She really isn't well at all. He's here all the time. He must sleep on the couch in the coffee room."

I think of Phil and how he waited impatiently for an answer that would push me far away.

"I was just fooling around—I didn't mean it, any of it," I mumbled finally, and watched his shoulders slowly sag with relief.

"You've got to be careful," he said, smiling easily. "Can't go around putting things on paper you don't mean."

Rachel looks distractedly at her hands. Then, just as quickly, she's happy again. "I've been so lucky," she says. "In Chicago, thirty years ago, we opened in *La Traviata,* and I played Violetta." She raises her eyes, looks directly at me. "Are you familiar with *Traviata,* Ardis?"

I nod my head. I must not look away. Frail Violetta, ill with a fatal disease, sings her lungs out until Act IV and then dies, her grief-stricken lover at her bedside.

"Do you remember," Rachel continues evenly, "the meltingly beautiful love songs? Alfredo was played by a young tenor from Boston. What a voice! What a man!"

She startles me then with what I would never have expected to hear in this sad place: a voice such as hers, still beautiful. She sings, *"A quell'amor ch'e palpito, dell'universo intero…"* It's the best section of the best aria and you always have to wait three minutes for Violetta to finally get there. How could Rachel have known that, out of the whole opera, this is the place where I'd like to lie down and live forever, even though it lasts only a minute and forty-five seconds. She finishes and sighs. Mom sighs. I'm barely breathing. She says in English, "That love, the pulse of the whole world… mysterious, unattainable. The torment. And delight!" Even her laughter is musical. "And *delight* of my heart!" She sighs again, dramatically, playfully, and winks at me.

My mother, laughing, crying, reaches over and energetically pats my hand. Suddenly I feel absurdly happy.

For Mom and Rachel and me, time has stopped on a heartbeat. There is no before, no after. We aren't any age, yet we are all ages. And there is no death. Only us, each somebody's daughter, three conspirators on the battlefield of love.

Activities   DYING FOR LOVE

■ Content and Style

1. a) List five words from the story that you have trouble understanding.

   b) In a group of three, compare your lists. Combine them into a glossary for the story. Use a dictionary to help you write a brief definition of each word.

2. a) Make a point-form outline of each of the two plots in this story:
   • Ardis at School
   • Ardis at the Hospital

b) Write a paragraph explaining how Ardis's experience with her mother and Rachel affect the feeling of "dying for love" that she has for Philip Chester.

3. In the fifth paragraph of the story, Ardis says, "The tragedy of real life is that the prime causes of personal anguish are often hilarious to lookers-on."

   a) Write an explanation of how this sentence is important to the story.

   b) As a class, brainstorm real life examples of this statement and then, on your own, write a story based on one of them.

■ Social Context

4. a) With a partner, reread the first two paragraphs of the story and answer the following questions:
   • What does Ardis tell the reader about herself?
   • What kind of person does she seem to be?
   • Is your first impression of Ardis positive or negative? Why?
   • What three questions would you like to ask her?
   b) Write Ardis a letter giving her advice about how to cope with her feelings towards Phil.

5. Make point-form notes on what Ardis says about her mother. In a paragraph, explain whether her opinion of her mother stays the same or changes. Use details from the story to support your opinion.

■ Personal and Imaginative Response

6. In a group of three, write a script of the conversation between Phil and Ardis the day after her visit to the hospital. Perform it for the class.

7. Ask your music teacher or librarian to help you find a plot outline of *La Traviata*. Write a paragraph explaining whether this story would appeal to today's youth.

Meg's First Day

BY DEBORAH KENT

I had practiced the walk to school three times the week before with Mom and my brother Sam, and the principal had even given me special permission to enter the building and learn where my classes would be held. Now, at the corner, I paused to review my directions: left on Prospect to the corner of Willow, across the street and left again down the long hill to Mulberry, across Mulberry, and half a block more to the signpost that marked the entrance to Ridge View High School. I used to envy Sam, his walks to school—friends ringing the doorbell, the group growing larger and noisier as it neared the school yard. From my bench on the front porch I would listen to them, running through the piles of dry leaves in the fall, throwing snowballs in the winter, teasing each other and making jokes about their teachers until their voices faded up the street.

The school bus was never like that. I would sit in the corner of my seat, reading a book or losing myself in daydreams, trying to draw away from the hubbub around me. No one had ever said so, but I was always sure that only weird kids had to take a bus and go to special school. The friends I made there never seemed as good as Sam's friends, who lived in the neighborhood, who could come over after school to play or do homework. There were voices ahead of me as I walked down the hill, the light, laughing voices of girls my own age.

"That's not what she told me," said the one on the right. "She told me he hung up on her."

"Yeah, but Sue, you can never believe what she says. She just likes to go after sympathy."

"I think she was telling the truth," said the one called Sue. Her voice was a little deeper and huskier than her friend's. "She was real upset, crying and all."

Suddenly I was afraid that they would turn and discover me behind them. Had they ever before seen someone who was blind? The rumble of traffic ahead told me that I was nearing Mulberry Street. I tried to tap my cane more lightly, left, right, left, right, assuring me of a clear path in front of me.

The girls had stopped, and I drew up beside them. "Paula's like that, though," Sue's friend said. "She can really put on a big act, and then..." However, her voice trailed off, and I felt them staring at me. My cane rang against the pavement. The tip dropped down to the street. I put out my foot and found the curb.

"Hi," I said into the silence.

A hand grasped my left wrist. "Careful," said Sue. "This is a real busy street."

"Are you going to school?" I asked as she propelled me forward.

"Yeah, are you?"

"Yes," I said, and I could think of nothing at all to add. What was Sue thinking, what was she wondering about me? If I could find the right words maybe I could put her at ease, maybe I could restore life to their conversation and it would go on where it had broken off, only now I would be part of it. I would find out about Paula and the boy who hung up on her. I would make them see that I was just another fifteen-year-old starting high school today—a little scared, but everybody was scared, and maybe we were all really worried about the same things.

"I can walk by myself," I said at the far curb, and pulled my arm free. For a few moments no one spoke, and my words echoed in my ears, too harsh, too resentful.

Still, when Sue's friend asked finally, "How are you going to manage?" I felt a flash of anger.

"Manage what?"

"Oh, you know—getting to classes, and what the teacher puts on the board—all that stuff."

I was explaining about visiting the school, about my Braille books, about being able to manage just fine, when Sue cried, "Darlene! Darlene, you nut, where've you been all summer?"

Then they were dashing ahead, melting into the laughing, chattering crowd that swarmed along the sidewalk. I felt like the only outsider as I pressed into the throng, alone and silent in the babble of greetings and gossip, clumsy and conspicuous with my white cane and my enormous book bag. I wished I had let Sam come with me after all.

I never found the signpost. As I searched for it through the crowd, my cane tangled among hurrying feet, and a boy exclaimed, "Why don't you watch where you're going?" But the signpost was quite unnecessary. I let the crowd sweep me around the turn, up the walk and through the heavy double front doors of Ridge View High School.

A week ago the corridor had stretched wide and empty, an avenue that lay so straight and clear I longed for a pair of roller skates. I could feel its height and width by the echoes my footsteps set bouncing from the walls and ceiling, and I walked a true course directly down the center. I had known that on this first morning it would not be the same, but nothing had prepared me for this frantic confusion. In the jostling crush of bodies I abandoned the use of my cane and fought ahead with one hand outstretched.

I don't know how I found the stairwell at the end of the hall. A bell rang, and feet thundered around me on the hollow treads. At least, I assured myself, no one had time to stare at me, to notice my uncertain steps and outstretched hand. At least for the moment I was no different from everyone else.

My homeroom, Two-Fourteen, was the third door on the right on the second-floor hall. A week ago I had found it easily by sliding my hand over the tall metal lockers and counting the doorways. But today I couldn't even reach the wall. I counted my steps and listened for clues, but my feet grew more and more unsure. At first I was afraid that I hadn't walked far enough, then that I had passed the door, and at last I seized a shoulder that brushed past me, and asked, "Where's Room Two-Fourteen?"

"This is Two-Twelve right here." It was a girl's voice, thin and nasal, with the hint of a whine.

"I must have passed it then." I turned back, so flustered that I forgot to thank her.

But she followed me protectively. "It must be this one," she said, grasping my arm just above the elbow. "Yeah, Two-Fourteen you wanted, right? This is it right here."

"Thanks," I said. I tried to free myself, to enter Two-Fourteen firmly on my own this first morning, but her fingers fastened more tightly and she pushed me ahead of her into the room. "I'm okay," I insisted, but she propelled me farther, and I was sure that the eyes of the entire class were fixed upon us.

"Here's a seat for you," she said. Her voice was loud in the relative quiet. "It's the first seat in the first row. That'll be easier for you." Her fingers relaxed their grip; she was gone.

Suddenly I realized that my book bag had grown very heavy. I set it down, folded my cane into its four short sections, and sank onto the hard plastic seat. My heart was pounding, and my hands were clammy with sweat.

All in all, it wouldn't have been a bad day if it hadn't been for the cafeteria. Students shouted and shoved, laughed and cursed. All of the regulations of Ridge View High were not enough to establish order there.

"Let me help you." It was a girl's voice, light and friendly. Gratitude overcame my desire for independence, and I was glad to let her maneuver me through the crowd. "Here's the end of the line," she said. "I've already got my tray, or I'd go through it with you. Can you make it from here?"

"Sure. Thanks."

Ahead of me two boys were deep in a discussion of the football team, and I followed them closely as the line crept forward. At last I heard the clatter of silverware just ahead. I found the stack of plastic trays, still hot and moist from recent washing, and hunted for the bins of knives and forks. "Come on! Move it!" a girl grumbled behind me. I grabbed a handful of silverware and slid my tray along the track.

"Hey," I said to the boy ahead of me, "can you tell me what there is here to eat?"

"All kinds of slop. You don't want any." His tray moved on and I followed, wondering miserably what I was passing up. The hiss of frying and the cloud of steam wafting from behind the counter told me we had reached the hot section. "Gimme some of that," the boy said; and I knew that I was next.

"What do you want?" the thin, cracked voice of an elderly woman demanded.

"I…I don't know. What is there?"

There was a moment of stunned silence before she burst out, "Oh, I'm so sorry, honey! I didn't realize! You like succotash? Let me give you some of this nice succotash. And how about some chicken croquettes? I'll give you a couple extra. I'm so sorry!"

But the worst part of all was still to come. At the cash register I realized that I still had to find a seat. The boys had dashed ahead, and I had lost their voices in the din. I thought of asking the girl behind me for help, but when I remembered her rough impatience, I was determined to go on alone. Hoisting my tray with one hand and wielding my cane with the other, I abandoned the safety of the line and entered the dining room.

"Is there an empty seat here?" I asked of anyone who might listen when my cane encountered a table leg.

"No," was the concise reply. Waxed paper rattled, a fork scraped a plate. I stood indecisively, taking in the sounds around me, trying to guess which way I should go. "There's a seat over there," a boy said finally.

"Over where?"

"Right over there. Over there on your left."

"Thanks," I made a sharp left turn and had taken two steps when the collision occurred. The tray leaped from my grasp, and I went down to shouts and the sound of shattering crockery. Inevitably someone cried, "Are you hurt?" and several demanded,

"What happened?" Dazed and wretched, I sat on the floor amid the ruins of my lunch and my pride.

"Well," Dad asked at the dinner table, "how was your big day?"

"Fine," I said, and then, in case he might not believe me, "It was a little rough at first with so many kids."

"Did you get a lot of homework?" Sam wanted to know.

"Tons! I never got this much last year."

"Do you need me to read anything to you?" Mom asked.

"No, I'm okay. I even got started in study hall. Everything is working out fine," I paused, remembering the girls on the street. "I just wish everybody'd quit trying to be so darn helpful all the time."

"They don't know what you can do and what you can't do," Dad said. "You're going to have to educate them."

"But they really bug me, you know," I said. "I can understand the kids maybe, but you'd think the teachers at least would be a little smarter."

"You'll just have to be patient," Mom said. As usual, she sided with Dad. "They've never known anyone before who was blind, and they're just trying to be nice."

"Nice!" I grumbled. Of course Dad and Mom were probably right, but that still didn't make it any easier. Only in the cafeteria, when I really did need someone, had no one offered assistance, and I had been too proud to ask. Maybe I was expecting people to read my mind.

"I've got the meanest math teacher," Sam said. "She's giving us twenty examples every night!"

"My history teacher's giving us a quiz every Friday," I said with a certain pride. "And in English we have to write a composition every week."

When dinner was over I followed Mom into the kitchen and started rinsing the plates. For a while we worked together in silence, putting the food away and loading the dishwasher. So I was caught off guard when she asked with sudden urgency, "How do you really feel about school?"

"I'm glad I'm there," I said. There was a lot I wasn't telling her, but that much, at least, was true.

■ Content and Style

1. a) Make a chart similar to the one below. Fill in the chart the way you think Meg would.

What I Like and Dislike About Ridge View High

Good Things	Bad Things

b) In a paragraph, explain why you would or would not want to stay at Ridge View High if you were Meg.

2. If you were this author, would you tell the story of Meg's first day at high school from the first-person point of view? Explain why or why not using examples from the story.

■ Social Context

3. With a partner, decide whether Meg's main struggle is external (with her environment) or internal (with herself). Present your conclusions to the class.

4. Write about a time when you felt a conflict between wishing for independence and needing help.

5. In a letter to Meg, provide some suggestions about how she might teach her fellow students to understand her needs.

■ Personal and Imaginative Response

6. a) With a partner, write the directions that a person who is blind would need to go from your classroom to one of the following places: the gym, the cafeteria, or the library. Use senses other than sight to make up your directions.

b) Trade your directions with those of another pair of students. Imagine that one of you is blind. Try to follow the directions as read out by your partner. After the walk, write about what happened.

7. As Meg, continue the story after two months in your new school. Connect some of your events with ones from the original story. Include both narration and dialogue.

On the Bridge

BY TODD STRASSER

"I beat up this guy at the mall yesterday," Adam Lockwood said. He was leaning on the stone wall of the bridge, smoking a cigarette and watching the cars speed by on the highway beneath him. His black hair fell down into his eyes.

"How come?" Seth Dawson asked, leaning on the stone wall next to him.

Adam shrugged. The turned-up collar of his leather jacket rose and fell along his neck. "He just bugged me, that's all. He was bigger, probably a senior. I guess he thought he could take me 'cause I was smaller. But I don't let anyone push me around."

"What'd you do to him?" Seth asked. He too was smoking a cigarette. It was his first ever, and he wasn't really inhaling. Just holding the smoke in his mouth for a while and then blowing it out.

"I'm pretty sure I broke his nose," Adam said. "I couldn't hang around to find out because the guy in the pizza place called the cops. I'm already in enough trouble with them."

"What for?" Seth asked. He noticed that when Adam took a drag, he seemed to hold the smoke in his mouth and then blow it out his nose. But it was probably just a different way of inhaling. Adam definitely inhaled.

"They just don't like me," Adam said. "You know how it is."

Seth nodded. Actually, he didn't know how it was. But there was no way he'd admit that. It was just pretty cool to think that the cops didn't like you. Seth was pretty sure the cops didn't even know who he was.

The two boys looked back down at the highway. It was a warm spring afternoon, and instead of taking the bus home after school, they'd decided to walk to the diner. There Adam had instructed Seth on how to feed quarters into the cigarette machine and get a pack of Marlboros. Seth had been really nervous about getting caught, but Adam told him it was no sweat. If the owner came out, you'd just tell him you were picking them up for your mother.

Now the pack of Marlboros was sticking out of the breast pocket of Seth's new denim jacket. It wasn't supposed to look new because he'd ripped the sleeves off and had washed it in the washing machine a hundred times to make it look old and worn. But somehow it had come out looking new and worn. Seth had decided to wear it anyway, but he felt like a fraud. Like a kid trying to imitate someone truly cool. On the other hand, Adam's leather jacket looked authentically old and worn. The right sleeve was ripped and the leather was creased and pliant. It looked like he'd been in a hundred fights with it. Seth had never been in a fight in his life. Not a serious punching fight, at least.

The other thing about Adam was, he wore the leather jacket to school every day. Adam wasn't one of these kids who kept their cool clothes in their lockers and only wore them in school because their parents wouldn't let them wear them at home. Seth had parents like that. His mother would have had a fit if she ever saw him wearing his sleeveless denim jacket, so he had to hide it in the garage every day before he went into the house. Then in the morning when he left for school he'd go through the garage and pick it up.

Seth leaned forward and felt the smooth cold granite of the bridge with his fingers. The bridge was old and made of large granite blocks. Its heavy stone abutments stood close to the cars that sped past on the highway beneath it. Newer bridges were made of steel. Their spans were longer and the abutments were farther from the road.

On the highway, a red Fiat convertible approached with two girls riding in the front seat. Adam waved, and one of the girls waved back. A second later the car shot under the bridge and disappeared. He turned to Seth and grinned. "Maybe they'll get off on the exit ramp and come back," he said.

"You think?" Seth asked. Actually, the thought made him nervous. "They must be old enough at least to drive."

"So?" Adam asked. "I go out with older girls all the time."

"Really?" Seth asked.

"Sure," Adam said. He took another drag off his cigarette and blew the smoke out of his nose. Seth wanted to try that, but he was afraid he'd start to cough or do something else equally uncool.

In the distance a big semitrailer appeared on the highway. Adam raised his arm in the air and pumped his fist up and down. The driver responded with three loud blasts of his air horns. A moment later the semi rumbled under them and disappeared.

"Let me try that," Seth said. Another truck was coming and he leaned over the stone ledge and jerked his arm up and down. But the trucker ignored him.

Adam laughed.

"How come it didn't work?" Seth asked.

"You gotta do it a special way," Adam told him.

"Show me," Seth said.

"Can't, man," Adam said. "You just have to have the right touch. It's something you're born with."

Seth smirked. It figured. It was just his luck to be born without the touch that made truckers blow their horns.

The traffic was gradually getting thicker as the afternoon rush hour approached. Many of the drivers and passengers in the cars seemed unaware of the two boys on the overpass. But a few others stared up through their windshields at them.

"Bet they're wondering if we're gonna drop something on them," Adam said. He lifted his hand in the air as if he was holding an imaginary rock. On the highway more of the people in the cars were watching now. Suddenly Adam threw his arm forward. Even though there was nothing in his hand, a woman driving a blue Toyota put her hands up in fear. Her car swerved momentarily out of its lane.

Seth felt his jaw drop. He couldn't believe Adam had done that. If the car had been going faster it might have gone out of control and crashed into the stone abutment next to the highway.

Meanwhile Adam grinned at him. "Scared her to death."

"Maybe we ought to go," Seth said, suddenly worried that they were going to get into trouble. What if a cop had seen them? Or what if the woman was really mad?

"Why?" Adam asked.

"She could get off and come back here."

Adam shrugged. "Let her," he said. "The last person in the world I'd be afraid of is some old lady." He took a drag off his cigarette and turned away to watch the cars again.

Seth kept glancing toward the exit ramp to see if the woman in the blue Toyota had gotten off. He was really tempted to leave, but

he stayed because he liked being with Adam. It made him feel good that a cool guy like Adam let him hang around.

A few minutes passed and the blue Toyota still did not appear on the exit ramp. Seth relaxed a little. He had smoked his Marlboro almost all the way down to the filter and his mouth tasted awful. Smoke kept getting in his eyes and making them water. He dropped the cigarette to the sidewalk and crushed it under his sneaker, relieved to be finished with it.

"Here's the way to do it," Adam said. He took the butt of his cigarette between his thumb and middle finger and flicked it over the side of the bridge and down into the traffic. With a burst of red sparks it hit the windshield of a black Camaro passing below. Adam turned and grinned. Seth smiled back uncomfortably. He was beginning to wonder just how far Adam would go.

Neither of them saw the black Camaro pull off onto the exit ramp and come up behind them on the bridge. Seth didn't notice it until he heard a door slam. He turned and saw three big guys getting out of the car. They were all wearing nylon sweatsuits, and they looked strong. Seth suddenly decided that it was time to go, but he quickly realized that the three guys had spread out, cutting off any way to escape. He and Adam were surrounded.

"Uh, Adam." Seth nudged him with his elbow.

"Wha–?" Adam turned around and looked shocked. In the meantime the three big guys were coming closer. Seth and Adam backed against the bridge wall. Seth felt his stomach tighten. His heart began to beat like a machine gun. Adam looked pretty scared too. Was it Seth's imagination, or was his friend trembling?

"Which one of you twerps flicked that butt on my car?" The question came from the husky guy with a black moustache and long black hair that curled behind his ears.

Seth and Adam glanced at each other. Seth was determined not to tell. He didn't believe in squealing on his friends. But suddenly he noticed that all three guys were staring at him. He quickly looked at Adam and saw why. Adam was pointing at him.

Before Seth could say anything, the husky guy reached forward and lifted him off the ground by the collar of his jacket. His feet kicked in the air uselessly for a second and then he was thrown against the front fender of the Camaro. He hit with a thud and lost his breath. Before he had a chance to recover, the guy grabbed him by the hair and forced his face toward the windshield.

"Lick it off," he grumbled.

Seth didn't know what he was talking about. He tried to raise his head, but the husky guy pushed his face closer to the windshield. God, he was strong.

"I said, lick it."

Lick what? Seth wanted to shout. Then he looked down at the glass and saw the little spot of grey ash where Adam's cigarette had hit. Oh, no. He stiffened. The thought made him sick. He tried to twist his head around, but the guy leaned his weight against Seth and pushed his face down again.

"Till it's clean," the guy said, pressing Seth's face down until it was only a couple of centimetres from the smooth, tinted glass. Seth stared at the little spot of ash. With the husky guy's weight on him, he could hardly breathe. The car's fender was digging into his ribs. Where was Adam?

The husky guy leaned harder against him, squeezing Seth painfully against the car. He pushed Seth's face down until it actually pressed against the cool glass. Seth could feel a spasm in his

29

chest as his lungs cried for air. But he clamped his mouth closed. He wasn't going to give the guy the satisfaction of seeing him lick that spot.

The husky guy must have known it. Suddenly he pulled Seth's head up, then slammed it back down against the windshield. *Wham!* Seth reeled backwards, his hands covering his nose and mouth. Everything felt numb, and he was certain his nose and some teeth were broken. He slipped and landed in a sitting position, bending forward, his throbbing face buried in his hands.

A second passed and he heard someone laugh. Looking up he saw the three guys get back into the Camaro. The car lurched away, leaving rubber.

"You're bleeding." Adam was standing over him. Seth took his hand away from his mouth and saw that it was covered with bright red blood. It was dripping down from his nose and chin onto his denim jacket, leaving red spots. At the same time he squeezed the bridge of his nose. It hurt, but somehow he knew it was not broken after all. He touched his front teeth with his tongue. They were all still there, and none felt loose.

"You want a hand?" Adam asked.

Seth nodded and Adam helped pull him up slowly. He was shaky on his feet and worried that his nose was going to start bleeding again. He looked down and saw that his denim jacket was covered with blood.

"I tried to help you," Adam said, "but one of them held a knife on me."

Seth glanced at him.

"It was a small knife," Adam said. "I guess he didn't want anyone to see it."

Seth felt his nose again. It was swollen and throbbed painfully. "Why'd you point at me?" he asked.

"I figured I could jump them if they made a move at you," Adam said. "How could I know they had knives?"

Seth shook his head. He didn't believe Adam. He started to walk toward home.

"You gonna make it okay?" Adam asked.

Seth nodded. He just wanted to be alone.

"I'll get those guys for you, man," Adam said. "I think I once saw one of them at the diner. I'm gonna go back there and see. Okay?"

Seth nodded again. He didn't even turn to watch Adam go.

On the way to his house, Seth stopped near some garbage cans a neighbour had put on the curb for collection. He looked down at his denim jacket. The spots of blood had turned dark. If he took it home and washed it now, the stains would probably make it look pretty cool. Like a jacket that had been worn in tons of fights. Seth smirked. He took it off and threw it in the garbage can.

Activities ON THE BRIDGE

■ Content and Style

1. Copy the chart below into your notebook. Write how you feel about each of the main characters before and after the incident with the Camaro. Note how the author makes you feel that way. Compare your chart with a partner's.

	Before the Incident	How the Author Creates These Feelings	After the Incident	How the Author Creates These Feelings
Adam				
Seth				

2. a) Adam says that one of the "three big guys" had a knife. Decide whether or not you believe him. Find support from the story for your opinion.

   b) As a class, divide into two groups: those who believe Adam and those who don't. Try to convince the opposite side that your opinion is correct. Use details from the story to support your position.

3. What sort of person do you think the author hopes will read "On the Bridge"? Write a paragraph to explain your ideas. Support your opinion with examples from the story.

■ Social Context

4. a) With a partner, describe what Adam and Seth are like.

   b) Decide which of the two would be labelled "cool" in your school.

   c) Think of the groups in your own school that stand out by the way they dress or act. Make a chart listing what each group thinks is cool.

5. a) As a class, brainstorm ideas about the following:
   - the qualities that allow some teenagers to have power over their peers
   - whether these teenagers usually put positive or negative pressure on their peers

   b) Write a letter to a Grade 7 or 8 student that gives advice about peer pressure.

■ Personal and Imaginative Response

6. Write the diary entry Seth or Adam might have made after the event on the bridge.

7. Imagine that you are a radio announcer reporting the event. Prepare and present a 30-second tape-recorded report on the event.

8. Draw a picture for a video jacket or a movie poster of this story. Make a series of thumbnail sketches that explore the different conflicts in the story. Choose your best sketch for the final product. Explain your artwork to the class.

Shinny Game Melted the Ice

BY RICHARD WAGAMESE

Back home they still call me "the one who went away."

Whenever the Wagamese family gets together, my uncles refer to me that way. They're old bush men, those uncles of mine and, having never really become comfortable with English, they lean more towards the Ojibway when talking about family. So, for them, I'll always be "the one who went away."

When I was four I disappeared. I vanished into the maw of the Ontario child welfare system. For 20 years the little family I left behind wondered if I was alive, where I was and what I was like. The man who walked back into their lives was vastly different from the fat-cheeked little boy who ran so carelessly through the bush.

It was hardest on my brother. My brother Charles, older, quieter, more refined than I, could never forget. It was he, who 20 years later, managed to track me down through Children's Aid Society records and bring me back home.

We don't get too much time to visit anymore. Jobs, geography and our personal lives keep us apart like grown-up brothers everywhere. Telephones, the odd letter scribbled in the midst of the daily scurry, infrequent visits and Christmas cards form the basis of our relationship these days.

I miss him. Despite the double decade absence we managed to reconnect to each other and there's a part of him that travels with me in everything.

One winter he hosted Christmas for the family. I travelled from out of the West and the rest of the Wagamese clan headed from Ontario to Charles' home in Saskatoon where he was a teacher in a native cultural survival school.

I arrived a few days before the rest and we had a chance to spend hours and hours together. One morning stands out through the years.

despite = malgrer.

It had snowed the night before and we were out early, standing in the frosty morning air, skates and sticks in hands, staring at the drifts that covered the neighborhood rink. It was apparent that industry alone would enable us to skate, so we dug into the task of clearing the rink.

Once it was finished, breath coming in thick clouds from our lungs, we still had the energy to race each other getting into our gear. This would be the first time we'd ever skated with each other, despite several long discussions about our mutual love of hockey. I was 26 and Charles was 29.

At first it was tentative. Our passes were soft, unchallenging and our strides loose, casual, smooth. We didn't talk much except to mutter the usual low, appreciative, monosyllabic asides like "nice," "good one," "great shot," perhaps the odd ooh and ah at something especially well done.

un syllabe

Nowadays I realize how very much it was like the development of our brotherhood.

Then someone—I don't recall which one of us it was—added a little hip as they swiped the puck from the other's stick. Soon the game became a frantic chase complete with bone-jarring checks, elbows, trips and over-the-shoulder taunts as we whirled around

provoquer

and around the rink, each other, and the unspoken effects of 20 years.

We must have kept it up for hours. Finally, we collapsed in a sweaty, exhausted heap at the blue-line, arms slapped around each other in what was arguably a clean check, sticks strewn across the ice and the puck a forgotten thing tucked away in the corner of the net.

We lay there for a long, long time laughing through our labored breathing, staring away across the universe. Brothers. Friends and playmates joined by something far deeper than a simple game of shinny. This was blood, rekindled, and renewed by the enthusiasm of a pair of boys disguised as men.

Neither of us cared what passers-by might think of a pair of native men hugging on the ice. Neither of us cared that the tears streaming down our cheeks might freeze, or that we'd have to walk home in wet blue jeans. All that mattered was that the disappeared years had finally melted down forever into this one hug between brothers who never had the chance to age together.

They call me "the one who went away." My family and I have had to work hard at repairing the damage caused by the Children's Aid decision of 1959. A lot of

34

Native families have. But the one
who went away is home and those
years have become a foundation
for our future.

I believe we become immortal
through the process of learning to
love the ones with whom we share
this planet. I believe that in the
heart of everyone who takes the
time to look, there's something
like that rink where we've chased
each others' dreams and lives
around, only to collapse in the
tears and laughter that will echo
forever across the universe.

And in this, we are all Indians.

I Lost My Talk

BY RITA JOE

I lost my talk
The talk you took away.
When I was a little girl
At Shubenacadie school.

You snatched it away:
I speak like you
I think like you
I create like you
The scrambled ballad, about my word.

Two ways I talk
Both ways I say,
Your way is more powerful.

So gently I offer my hand and ask,
Let me find my talk
So I can teach you about me.

■ Content and Style

1. a) In your notebook, describe what both authors lost by being separated from their families at a young age. Include details from the two selections.

   b) Compare your description with a partner's and add any points you may have missed.

2. As a class, discuss the ideas or themes that both "Shinny Game Melted the Ice" and "I Lost My Talk" have in common. Point out any words and phrases that help the reader to discover these themes.

■ Social Context

3. a) With a partner, define *identity* and *self worth*. List what you think is important to your identity and self worth. Consider personal qualities, values, activities, culture, family, and friends.

   b) Write a response to this statement and share it with class-mates:

   "It is important for young people to be involved in activities that help them establish their own identity and self worth."

4. a) As a class, explain the following:
   • why the narrator in the poem felt powerless at the school she attended
   • how finding her own talk would help her regain a sense of her own power

   b) With a partner, role play a visit the narrator might have made to a trusted older friend to talk about her feelings.

■ Personal and Imaginative Response

5. Recall or imagine a time when you moved to a place where you were not allowed to speak your own language or talk about your own culture. Write a letter to one of your friends, describing your feelings in this new environment.

My Mother

BY AFUA COOPER

My mother planted fields
married a man
bore ten children
and still found time
to run her own business
I remember once
She and I
were going to work
the plot of land
she rented from someone
we heard the missionary's car
coming down the road
she jumped over a culvert to hide
because she had on a pair
of my father's pants
the church disapproved of women
wearing men's clothing
when the sun was steadily going westward
we hurried from the field
she had to rush home
to cook the family's meal
she seemed able to do anything
and I think that in one
of her past lives
she was a leader of some sort

my mother planted fields
married a man
bore ten children
and still found time
to run her own business.

I Am Yours

Act One, Scene Nineteen

BY JUDITH THOMPSON

Characters
Pegs
Taxi Driver

Pegs: Your children are only loaned to you, that's what Muriel said; they're only loaned to you for a short time.... It comes as quite a shock to us, you know, us girls who been brought up to think family is our whole life and ya grow up and ya get married and ya start havin kids and you are in your prime, man, everybody on the street smiles, they respect ya, you're the most powerful thing there is, a mother, with young kids, and the kids think you're Christmas, they want to sit on your knee, and help ya bake cookies, Mum this, Mum that, and you're tired as hell but you're having the time of your LIFE, right? You're important, you're an important member of society, kids all around you, friend's kids, sister's kids, car pools, Round Robin—you're havin a ball! And then they get older, ya go back to work, and it's their friends, their friends are more important than you, than anything in the world, ya couldn't drag them out on a picnic for a million dollars, and it seems they only talk to you if it's to get money or the car. They whip through their meals in about ten seconds flat, something took you five hours of buying and chopping and mixing and cooking and then they leave the house. And ya never see em, and ya wonder if they hate you. You know they're only there because of the money thing, they'd be gone in a second if there was a chance. Why is that? Why don't they like you anymore? I tried; you know, I tried like hell to listen to the AC-DC and the Led Zepplin and all that, even said I liked it, I did

38

like that "Stairway to Heaven" one, I used to get jokes from the magazines, newspapers, you know, a Mum with a sense of humour? That went over like a lead balloon. I'd drive him to his parties, his roller skatin, his hockey and baseball, we'd go the whole drive silent, not a single word. Only word was at the end, "Pick me up at eight o'clock."…What happened? What happened to the baby who looked up at me with eyes when the doctor first showed him to me, blackberry eyes, the baby I musta walked ten miles a day in our little apartment, back and forth, back and forth, eyes closin, lookin at me, lookin at me. Why is it that look goes away?

Driver: Three seventy-five, please, lady?

Pegs: I know. I know how much it is.

Activities   MY MOTHER/I AM YOURS

■ Content and Style

1. a) In a group of four, choose one of these two selections and read it aloud twice.

   b) Make a chart of two columns in your notebook. In the first column, write any feelings you have as you listen to the reading. In the second column, write the words and/or phrases that make you feel that way.

   c) Discuss what you think is the main idea or theme of the selection. Be prepared to defend your opinion with details from the selection.

   d) Share your chart and theme ideas with groups that chose the other selection.

■ Social Context

2. With a partner, decide what Pegs is saying about motherhood in the script excerpt "I Am Yours." Role play a conversation she might have with her son.

39

3. Using "I Am Yours" as a model, write a monologue in which you express your feelings about being a son or daughter. You might include your thoughts about the following:
   - your sense of power/powerlessness in your family
   - your relationship with other members of your family

■ Personal and Imaginative Response

4. Think of an adult for whom you have a lot of respect. Write a letter to the person, explaining why you think so highly of her or him.

5. a) Choosing one of the two selections, develop a list of five or more questions you might ask the mother in an interview with her. Share your list with a partner.
   b) Choose five of your questions and, with a partner, take the roles of the interviewer and the mother. Write and perform the interview for classmates.

Words on a Page

BY KEITH LECKIE
BASED ON A STORY IDEA BY DANIEL MOSES

The idea for this screenplay came from Native writer Daniel Moses. Keith Leckie wrote it as an episode for the Spirit Bay *television series. Filmed on location on the Rocky Bay Reserve in northern Ontario, the series dramatizes the lives of the people of Spirit Bay, a small fictional Ojibway community on the shore of Lake Nipigon in the Canadian Shield.*

Characters
Lenore Green–an Ojibway teenager
Pete Green–Lenore's father, a fisher and trapper
Connie Green–Lenore's mother
Sadie Green–Lenore's younger sister
Miss Walker–Lenore's Grade 10 teacher
The Principal of Lenore's high school
Various Students
Driver
Man

ACT ONE
1. Int. Classroom. Day.
(It is a sunny fall afternoon in Lenore's Grade 10 English class. Sunrays through dust particles in the air. There are a dozen classmates, a mixture of white and Native, listening as Lenore reads a story she has written.)

Lenore: …So on that morning before she left, they went by canoe one last time to those favourite places. It was at first light, when the water is a mirror and the trees are still, as if nature is holding her breath.
(A variety of young faces listen, all enthralled with her story. Camera moves slowly, panning across the classroom holding on different faces.)

And there was the beaver and the loon and the hawk circling above the treetops. And below the trout and the sturgeon slipped silently through the black water.

(Camera stops on one Girl, listening intently, then moves again. Camera holds on two Boys slouching close together, almost touching, but their eyes and attention are on Lenore at the front of the class.)

Creatures as powerful as the great moose, as small as a minnow. She and her father took their place among them.

(Camera cuts to Miss Walker, the Native teacher. She sits to one side of Lenore listening as intently as the rest. She is very impressed. Camera pans and pulls focus to hold finally on Lenore as she finishes the story. She has memorized most of it and hardly has to look at the page. She speaks very well with skilled emphasis and a personal passion for her words.)

And in this world there was a peace and harmony that she knew no matter how far she travelled, she would never find again. She understood now why her father had brought her here. She felt the morning sun on her face and the gentle rocking of the canoe and smiled because she knew that here would always be her home.

(Lenore stops speaking, holds the few pages against her chest with both arms and looks at Miss Walker a little anxiously. There is a hushed silence for a moment.)

Miss Walker: *(Quietly)* Lenore, that was beautiful!

(Lenore gives a shy, tentative smile.)

What did you think, class?

(The class gives a collective chatter of positive response, then…)

Girl #1: It was real sad.

Boy #1: It reminded me of…like around Shadow River.

Girl #2: It was just like a book.

(There is a silent moment after this pronouncement. Lenore looks at the other students trying to suppress her excitement. The bell rings signalling the end of class and the students quickly exit the classroom. When the wave of students has passed, Lenore is left still standing there. Miss Walker puts a hand on her shoulder.)

Miss Walker: I'm really very impressed, Lenore. Leave your story on my desk. There are some people I'd like to show it to.

(Miss Walker then exits, leaving Lenore alone. She takes a deep breath then allows herself a beaming smile as she hugs her story against herself.)

2A. Ext. Stream. Afternoon.
(The prow of a cedar canoe cuts through the calm water. Lenore and her father, Pete, in the stern, are canoeing their way up a quiet stream. It is late in the afternoon. The shadows are lengthening, and the sunlight retains the shimmering intensity of this time of day as it filters through the autumn foliage.)

Pete: Good here for beaver. Heavy willow growth. Lots of food.
(Lenore notices a beaver swimming. She points.)

Lenore Look, Baba.
(Shot of beaver swimming. He suddenly slaps his tail loudly and dives—stock shot.)

He's warning his friends about us.

Pete: *(Seriously)* You know that a long time ago the beaver only had a little skinny tail.

Lenore: Oh yeah?
(Lenore looks back smiling expectantly. She knows this is the opening to one of her father's crazy stories.)

Pete: *(Storytelling tone)* You see, one day Nanabozho was out paddling his big canoe. He's pretty lazy so he decided if he gave the beaver a big paddle tail, he could tie them on the back and they would push his canoe. But once he had given the beaver a paddle tail, the beaver was too quick to catch. So he didn't get a chance to try it.

Lenore: *(Only half serious)* D'you think it would work?

Pete: Cheemo and I tried it once.

Lenore: Really?

Pete: Sure! Roped a couple 70-pound beavers on the back of his canoe.

Lenore: What happened?

Pete: Well, they chewed a hole in the canoe and we all sank and they got away!
(Lenore laughs at this image and turns to look back at her father.)

Lenore: Serves you right.
(Pete laughs too. They continue paddling slowly, quietly.)

2B. Ext. Beaver Pond. Day.
(They canoe near a bubbling beaver dam with more beaver houses visible.)

Pete: You said you had a dream to tell.

Lenore: Yes. *(She turns around in canoe, facing him.)* It's pretty simple, I guess. I'm standing in the woods. There's a raven flying just above my head. It hovers there. It has something to tell me. *(Pause, thinking)* It wants to land…but it can't. It only hovers there. It never lands.

(Pete thinks about the dream very seriously for a moment.)

Pete: Sounds like a good dream. Can't tell you what it means. Maybe it isn't finished with you yet. *(Lenore smiles. Pause)* You know Cheemo had the same dream for five nights in a row. He dreamed he was swimming underwater.

Lenore: Yeah?

Pete: Every night, same thing. Swimming underwater!

Lenore: Yeah?

Pete: On the sixth day, he couldn't stand it anymore. He jumped in the lake! And no more dream.

(They both laugh again.)

We'll go upstream to the next pond and…

Lenore: *(Hesitant)* Baba, I…

Pete: What?

Lenore: *(Feeling badly)* I've got all kinds of homework to do. We've got a lot of tests coming up…

Pete: Isn't it enough they have you all day at that school?

Lenore: I'm sorry, Baba.

Pete: *(Gruffly)* Never mind.

(Pete quickly backpaddles to turn the canoe around and they head back the way they came. Lenore looks unhappy.)

3. Ext. Schoolyard. Day.

(It is lunch break at school. A number of students are sitting around on the grass and walls eating lunch. Some play volleyball nearby. Lenore is sitting on a bench reading some poetry to a Classmate. Sadie, Lenore's sister, is listening in. Lenore reads with feeling from the book.)

Lenore:
"Up on the hill against the sky,
A fir tree rocking its lullaby,
Swings, swings

Its emerald wings,
Swelling the song that my paddle sings."

Classmate #1: That's neat!

Lenore: Yeah. Pauline Johnson. She's a Native poet who travelled all around these lakes almost 100 years ago. Musta been hard to get gas for her outboard then, eh?
(They laugh. Miss Walker comes up behind them with a letter in her hand. She crouches behind them.)

Miss Walker: *(Excited, smiling)* Lenore? I've got some news for you. I sent your story in to the District Writing Competitions. You've been accepted as a finalist!
(She shows Lenore the letter. Lenore and Sadie read it together. Lenore is both excited and disbelieving.)

Next week you go down to Thunder Bay to read your story to the judges!
(Lenore and Sadie look at each other in amazement.)

This is wonderful! If you do well there, they could send you to a special high school in the south. Then maybe to study English at university!

Lenore: *(Mixed emotions)* University!

Miss Walker: Well, let's see how Thunder Bay goes. We just need a letter of permission from your parents and we're all set!
(Lenore looks at the letter again, confused and excited. Miss Walker smiles at her, then leans forward and gives her a little hug.)

I'm proud of you.
(Miss Walker gets up and leaves them. Again Sadie and Lenore look at each other.)

Sadie: Nice going!

Lenore: *(Grinning)* Yeah! I can't believe it! *(Frowning)* I just wonder what Baba's going to say.

4. Int. Kitchen (Lenore's home). Evening.
(Lenore, Sadie, their mother, Connie, and Pete are having fish dinner. Pete eats his food hungrily. Lenore looks up at him once, then again. Then she notices Sadie staring at her impatiently. Lenore glares at Sadie and they both resume eating.)

Pete: *(To all)* Good trout, eh? We caught them way north of Mulligan Bay. Cold and deep.

(He takes another huge mouthful.)

Connie: We should have enough in the freezer to last until Christmas.

Pete: The King of France never ate better than this.
(There is a moment of silence. Sadie can wait no longer.)

Sadie: Baba, Lenore has something to ask you.
(Pete and Connie look up. Lenore glares at Sadie.)

Pete: Uh huh?
(Lenore bolsters her courage.)

Lenore: Well…I've been doing some work at school…

Pete: Yeah. So?

Lenore: You know…like writing.
(Pete takes another large bite of fish, only vaguely interested.)

Anyway…the new teacher, Miss Walker, said I've been doing real well…and there was a story I wrote…

Pete: A what?

Lenore: *(Hesitating)* Well, a story…and they, ah…

Sadie: *(Interrupting)* The story won a contest and now she has to go to Thunder Bay to read it and then they'll send her away to university!
(Lenore "looks daggers" at Sadie. Both Pete and Connie look at Lenore in surprise.)

Lenore: Can't you shut up!

Pete: University!
(Lenore passes Pete the letter.)

Lenore: Well no! It's only if I win, but…
(Pete glances at the letter then pushes it away.)

Pete: That's crazy! You're only a young girl! You can forget about going to Thunder Bay.

Lenore: But I have to! I'm representing the school!

Pete: They can find someone else.

Lenore: But they want my story!

Pete: Then send the story to Thunder Bay.

Lenore: *(Approaching tears)* But I want to go!!

Pete: "Want" and "Can" are not always the same thing.

(Pete goes back to his dinner.)

Lenore: You never..!

(Lenore is about to continue her argument but her mother is signalling her not to continue along these lines. Lenore stands up and quickly exits the kitchen.)

ACT TWO

5. Int. Classroom. Day.

(The classroom is empty except for Lenore standing at the front and Miss Walker sitting in a desk several rows back. Lenore is practising reading her story with a compelling intensity.)

Lenore: She found her father out behind the shed laying the steaming cedar strips across the frame of a new canoe, his strong hands molding the soft wood. "Baba," she said, "Why can't I visit Aunt Doreen for the summer? I'm not a child anymore. I want to ride a subway, Baba! I want to climb to the top of a skyscraper, and see a museum and go to a play. I want to see the world!" But her father turned away and would not look at her.

(Lenore stops and thinks about her father for a moment.)

Miss Walker: *(Quietly)* Yes. Go on.

(Suddenly all of Lenore's momentum is gone. She appears weary.)

Lenore: Can we stop now?

Miss Walker: Sure. Sure, that's fine. It's coming along really well, Lenore. Parents' Night will be a good rehearsal for the finals.

(Pause, looking at Lenore who appears distracted)

Is everything alright?

Lenore: Yes. I'm just tired.

Miss Walker: Good. You get a good sleep. I'll see you tomorrow.

(Lenore gives her a half-hearted smile and leaves the classroom. Miss Walker looks after her, wondering if there is anything wrong.)

6. Int. Kitchen (Lenore's house). Day.

(Lenore comes into the kitchen, tosses down her books and flops down at the table. Her mother is making bannock bread. They are alone. Her mother notices her unhappiness.)

Connie: How was school?

Lenore: Okay. *(Pause)* Actually it was lousy. *(Sudden anger)* I just don't understand! Why won't he let me go?!

(Connie stops work and sits down across from her.)

Connie: *(After a moment)* He is afraid of what will happen to you.

Lenore: He wants to trap me!

Connie: It might seem like that, but he believes he's protecting you.

Lenore: *(Deflated)* What am I going to do, Mum?

Connie: He's stubborn. The harder you push, the more he digs in his heels. *(Pause)* D'you remember the story of the Sun and the Wind, how they had a contest to see who could get the coat off a passing man? The Wind blew as hard as he could, but the man held the coat on tightly. When the Sun had his turn, he shone warm and bright and the man just took off his coat.

Lenore: I should be the sun?

(Connie nods.)

Connie: Maybe you can read your story to him.

Lenore: I have to read it on Parents' Night. But he'll never come.

Connie: Maybe this time, if you ask, he will.

(Lenore looks suddenly hopeful.)

Lenore: You think so?

Connie: *(Smiling)* Maybe.

(Lenore smiles happily.)

7. Ext. Woods. Day.

(A small cedar tree crashes to the ground near the banks of a stream. Pete stands beside the stump, axe in hand. He wipes a sleeve across his sweating forehead, then quickly begins to trim the branches.

With a smaller axe Lenore competently trims the branches of another downed cedar in the foreground. In the background we see a sturdy lean-to three-quarters completed, large enough to sleep two or three people with provisions—side walls, open front, firepit. Lenore lifts her ten-foot cedar pole, takes it to the structure and fits it in place, resting on the centre beam nailed between two trees.

Pete is suddenly beside her and places his pole beside hers, which almost completes the superstructure of the roof. He smiles at her.)

Pete: Now the tarp, a good layer of cedar boughs and one snowfall will make it warm and dry. Ron and I'll live here a week for trapping. *(Looking at her)* What d'you think? You want to come?

Lenore: Where?

Pete: Out on the new trapline in November with Ron and me?

Lenore: *(Excited)* Yeah! *(Then subdued)* But I've got school.
(Pete turns away to adjust the poles on the crosspiece.)
(Hopefully) But maybe I can get off for a couple of days.

Pete: *(Not looking at her)* You think about it.

8. Ext. Rocky Stream Bed. Day.
*(Lenore kneels down on a flat rock. Holding her hair back she drinks
from the surface of the black, bubbling stream. Camera at stream level.
She looks up, satisfied, her face wet. She watches her father who puts
his face right down in the water and shakes his head, splashing and
blowing bubbles. He looks up at her and they both laugh, water dripping off their faces.*
   *Pete cups some water in his hand and brings it to his lips to drink.
Lenore watches him a moment.)*

Lenore: Sometimes I wish I could be a son for you, Baba.
(Pete looks up at her curiously at this statement out of the blue.)

Pete: A son?

Lenore: Yes. I know every father wants a son.
(Pete considers this as he fills a canteen with water.)

Pete: I would like a son. Maybe someday… *(Pause)* but the first
time I saw you and you smiled at me, I wouldn't have traded you
for ten sons!
(Lenore smiles at this, watching him fill the canteen.)

Lenore: Baba?

Pete: Hummm?

Lenore: Parents' Night is on Wednesday.

Pete: *(Distastefully)* Parents' Night?!

Lenore: Yeah. I'm going to read something. Be real nice if you were
there.

Pete: I don't have anything to say to those teachers.

Lenore: You don't have to say anything.

Pete: *(Resisting)* And we're fishing the next day. We'll be outfitting
the boat.

Lenore: Just for a little while? Maybe? *(Pause)* Please?

Pete: Okay. I'm not promising but I'll try.
(Lenore smiles, her eyes sparkling.)

9. Ext. Open Sky (Dream). Day.
(In slow motion against a blue sky background a single bird comes into frame. Shot in slightly slow motion. It hovers above the camera. After a moment it is joined by other birds…two, three, four, all hovering in frame above the camera. It is not a threatening image. The motion is beautiful to watch. The sound of the wings becomes steadily louder.)

10A. Int. Lenore's Bedroom. Night.
(Lenore, with a little gasp, suddenly sits up in bed, staring out in front of her. Her tense body relaxes. She thinks for a moment about the images of the dream. She lays down again and rolls over, her face toward camera. She smiles with excitement and anticipation.)

10B. Ext. Spirit Bay Docks. Late Day.
(A pickup truck stops beside the docks. Pete is waiting. The Driver gets out and opens the tailgate.)

Driver: Got your new nets, Pete.
(Pete inspects the three bundles of nets as the Driver drops them on the ground.)

Pete: Hey, they don't have floats!
(The Driver hands him the bill.)

Driver: See? Nothing about floats.
(Pete looks at the bill. The Driver looks at him, then turns the bill right side up for him to read. Pete glances at it and stuffs it into his pocket.)

Pete: Gonna take me all night to sew floats on these nets.

Driver: You want 'em or not?
(Pete nods. The Driver drops the last net on the ground, gets back in the truck and drives off. As the truck drives away, Pete checks his watch, looks unhappy, then carries the first bundle toward the boat.)

11. Int. School Auditorium. Evening.
(It's Parents' Night in the small auditorium. There are about two dozen parents present, Native and white. Tables display artwork of various kinds and highly graded tests and essays. There is a coffee and pastry table where parents stand in small groups talking with four or five teachers.

There is a podium at the front of the auditorium. Lenore stands near it anxiously watching the doorway, holding the pages of her story.)

Sadie: Betcha he doesn't come.

Lenore: He'll come.

(Miss Walker approaches them.)

Miss Walker: Hi Lenore. Are you ready?

Lenore: *(Anxious)* I think so.

Miss Walker: You'll do great! Are your parents here yet? I was looking forward to meeting them.

Lenore: *(Eyeing the doorway)* They'll be here any minute.

(The Principal moves behind the podium to address those present. Conversation dwindles.)

Principal: Good evening, and welcome to the first Parents' Night of the year at Nipigon District Junior High School. Glad you could come out. In a moment I'll ask one of our students to come up and read a prize-winning story she's written...

(Principal's talk continues over dialogue between Lenore and Miss Walker, below.)

But first I would like to say a few words about the challenges facing us in the coming year. Never before has there been such an abundance of information and communication in our world...

(Lenore whispers anxiously to Miss Walker.)

Lenore: Wait! I can't do it yet!

Miss Walker: Don't worry. I'll stall him if necessary. *(Smiling)* Mr. Crankhurst goes on forever, anyway.

(Lenore tries to smile. She looks at the Principal.)

Principal: It is almost overwhelming when you consider it. In the face of this, a sound education has never been more important. And so, our goal will remain a high standard of academic achievement and individual excellence in all our endeavours. We are deeply aware of our responsibility here at Beardmore to mould the bright minds of young men and women who will in a few short years forge the destiny of our world!

(Connie comes through the door into the auditorium. She is alone. Lenore watches her. Connie stops, looks around the room and sees Lenore. She looks at her and shakes her head sadly. Pete is not coming. Lenore appears as if she's about to cry. Sadie takes this all in.)

So now let me introduce one of those bright young minds, to read her story that has been selected for the finals of the District Writing Competition...Lenore Green.

(There is polite applause. Lenore turns to Miss Walker in anger and frustration.)

Lenore: I'm not going to do it.

Miss Walker: *(Sudden alarm)* What!?

Lenore: Why bother!

(The applause dies out. The Principal and all others are looking expectantly at Lenore. With story in hand, Lenore turns and exits the auditorium. There are whispered comments in the audience of parents. Miss Walker quickly follows Lenore.)

12. Int. Hallway (School). Evening.
(The hallway is deserted. Lenore walks determinedly away from the auditorium. Miss Walker comes out the door and calls after her.)

Miss Walker: Lenore! Lenore!

(Lenore stops and turns back. Miss Walker comes up to her.)

What's wrong!? I don't understand.

Lenore: I don't want to read my story. And I don't want to go to Thunder Bay!

Miss Walker: But Lenore! This is a great opportunity! This is the first big step in your career.

Lenore: What career?!

Miss Walker: You could do anything—go to university, become a journalist or an English professor or a playwright. You've been given a talent. You can't turn your back on it!

Lenore: It's only a stupid story. I'm sorry I even wrote it.

(Lenore throws the story down on the floor, turns and walks away. After a beat Miss Walker reaches down and picks up the spilled pages. She looks at them, then watches Lenore walking away from her.)

ACT THREE

13. Int. Classroom. Morning.
(Miss Walker is sitting at her desk marking tests in the empty classroom. She works quickly for a moment, but then her momentum slows, her eyes leave her work and brows knitted she begins to think again about Lenore. She can't figure it out.

    Sadie and Connie enter the room behind her. Connie is intimidated by a woman of her own generation with a university education. She looks uncomfortably around the room.)

Sadie: Miss Walker?

Miss Walker: *(Turns around and stands)* Hi Sadie…and Mrs. Green. How are you?

(Connie nods shyly. It takes a moment to find the words, but she speaks them with determination.)

Connie: There is something you should know. Lenore loves to write more than anything. And she wants to go to Thunder Bay. But my husband… *(A little ashamed)* he won't let her.

Sadie: Baba doesn't believe in schools and books and stuff.

Miss Walker: *(Reflectively)* I see. Please sit.

(Miss Walker gestures to a chair for Connie and another for Sadie.)

14A. Ext. Spirit Bay Docks. Afternoon.
(Pete is unloading his catch after a good day's fishing. He is on the dock. A Crewman hands him a tub full of ice and fish from the deck on the boat. There are several tubs on the dock.)

Pete: *(Feigning pain)* Uhhh! The only trouble with a good catch is it's bad for my back!

(The Crewman laughs.

Pete lifts the tub of fish and walks a few steps to the other tubs when he notices Lenore. Lenore stands—with school books—at the far end of the dock watching Pete from a distance. Other students pass by behind her on their way home. Lenore and Pete look at each other a moment. Pete puts the tub down with the others and wiping his hands with a rag takes a step toward her. Lenore turns and quickly walks away. Pete stops and watches her, feeling badly.)*

14B. Int. Classroom. Afternoon.
(Connie and Sadie are talking to Miss Walker. Connie is more relaxed now. She is reflective.)

Connie: When I was Lenore's age, I was real good at school too. Top of my class. I might have gone on to university, even! But I couldn't decide…and then I met Pete… *(Pause, then with conviction)* I want this for Lenore!

Miss Walker: So do I.

Connie: We're having a roast Sunday. Why don't you come by?

(Connie and Miss Walker and Sadie share a conspiratorial smile.)

Miss Walker: Good! I will.

15. Ext. Lenore's House. Day.
(Establishing shot/time passage. A car and a pickup truck are parked outside.)

16. Int. Kitchen (Lenore's House). Day.
(The table is nicely laid out with flowers and a bright, plastic tablecloth and a variety of food—fish, slices of moose, potatoes and other vegetables, and bannock bread. Miss Walker sits at one end of the table, Pete at the other. Sadie and Connie sit on one side, Lenore on the other.

Lenore is very quiet. She is angry at her father and embarrassed by Miss Walker being there. She is uncomfortable to be at the table with both of them. Miss Walker takes a platter of meat from Lenore.)

Miss Walker: Thanks Lenore.
(Pete is eating his food hungrily, eyes on his plate. Miss Walker is talking mostly to Connie, though she watches Pete for any response.)

…and we're getting in a new portable classroom and adding to the library…
(Pete without looking up grunts his disfavour over this.)

And what I'm hoping for by the end of the year is a computer terminal for the students to use…

Pete: *(Grunts again)* Pass the moose.
(Miss Walker finds the platter of moose beside her and passes it. Pete piles moose meat on his plate. Miss Walker looks at him, is about to say something to him, then thinks better of it.)

Miss Walker: One thing I'm excited about *(She looks at Pete)*…and Mr. Crankhurst seems open to it…is an Ojibway Studies course.
(Pete looks up at this.)

Pete: *(With disdain)* Ojibway Studies?

Miss Walker: Yes. The language and customs and history…

Pete: Like one of them dead civilizations in a museum.

Miss Walker: No! Not at all. In fact, you trap and fish. Maybe you'd come in and give demonstrations of your expertise?

Pete: Expertise! If you get paid by the word, that's a ten dollar one for sure!
(Sadie giggles at this. Miss Walker is angry. The gloves are off.)

Miss Walker: I can see you don't think much of education, but it can give all kinds of things to a girl like Lenore.

55

Pete: You mean like a one-way ticket out of here.

(Miss Walker takes out the folded pages of Lenore's story and unfolds them.)

Miss Walker: Have you read this?

Pete: No.

(Connie looks worried.)

Miss Walker: Well I think you should read it!

Pete: *(Suddenly awkward)* I will…later.

Miss Walker: Read it now! Just the first page.

(She stands up, reaches over and puts the manuscript down in front of him. Pete moves it away. Miss Walker stays standing.)

Pete: No.

Miss Walker: Well if you don't care enough to even read…

(Pete stands up angrily.)

Pete: You saying I don't care about my daughter?!

Miss Walker: She has talent and imagination and desire! You can't imprison her here!

Pete: Prison!!

Miss Walker: There's a whole world waiting for her out there!

(Lenore sits there becoming angry and frustrated listening to this.)

Pete: In that world she'll be an outsider! She'll be alone and unhappy and forget who she is!

(Lenore stands up and looks at Pete.)

Lenore: You don't know who I am! *(Then at Miss Walker)* Neither of you! No one even cares what I want!

(Lenore turns away and exits the house. Pete and Miss Walker look at each other, now sorry that they have been so insensitive.)

17. Ext. End of Dock (Sunset Lodge). Day.
(Lenore crouches on the end of the dock. She looks down at her reflection in the black water. She holds out a pebble and lets it drop into the reflection. When it clears a moment later, her father's reflection can be seen behind. He stands there a moment.)
Lenore: *(Residual anger)* Why won't you read my story?
(Pete crouches down beside her and looks out at the water a moment. He doesn't look at her as he speaks.)
Pete: Because…I can't.

(Lenore looks at him in surprise.)

I never learned to read so good. You never knew, eh?

(Lenore shakes her head, pause, then bitterly)

When I went to school there was a teacher…If I didn't learn my lessons or talked Indian, he'd beat me with a switch and call me names. One day I took the switch away from him and never went back. Never been in a school since.

(Lenore watches her father, her expression softening.)

Lenore: Come for a walk?

(Pete looks up at her for the first time, smiles and nods.)

18A. Ext. Spirit Bay Field. Day.
(A telephoto lens shows Pete and Lenore walking side by side toward camera. The background shows the picturesque village of Spirit Bay on the edge of the lake. They walk in silence for a moment.)

Pete: I'm afraid. *(Pause)* Afraid that you'll go away and become a stranger to us.

Lenore: How could I do that?!

Pete: If you go south to school. It's very different there.

18B. Ext. Spirit Bay Road. Day.
(Pete and Lenore walk toward camera, telephoto lens.)

Lenore: I'll always be Nishnabe, Baba. And Spirit Bay is my home.

Pete: Others have said that and not come back.

Lenore: I'll come back! I want to learn to write better so I can live here and tell about our people! That's why I want to write!

(Pete thinks about this hard as they walk along. They fall silent again.)

19. Ext. Dreamer's Rock. Afternoon.
(Pete and Lenore sit atop Dreamer's Rock facing the lake that stretches out before them to the horizon. The village can be seen below, and distant islands in the lake.)

Lenore: I've been waiting to tell you the last of the dreams. The dreams of the bird that wants to land.

Pete: *(Very interested)* Yes! Is it finished?

Lenore: It's finished.

Pete: How did it end?

Lenore: Remember I told you the bird was hovering and trying to land? *(Pete nods)* Well then each night there were more birds—a few and then dozens…then hundreds of birds! *(Pause, remembering)* And there was a wide open field of snow! And there they began to land, black against the white snow.
(Pete is listening intently.)

Pete: They all landed?

Lenore: Yes! And as each bird landed it became a letter. And the snow was like a page. And the bird-letters formed words. And the words sentences. *(Looking at him)* They were my words, Baba! They were the words I wrote!
(Lenore stops, thinking about the images. Pete smiles at her, excited by the dream but saddened by its meaning.)

Pete: Sounds like you are meant to be a writer. I won't stop you.
(Lenore is not satisfied.)

Lenore: But I need more, Baba. I don't know if I can do it alone. I need your help.

Pete: *My* help? I can't even read!

Lenore: Not that kind. I need your… *(Pause, finding right word)* courage. Will you come to Thunder Bay and hear me read my story?

Pete: *(Unhappily)* At the university?!
(Lenore nods. Pete hesitates, then answers.)

I'll come.
(Lenore takes his hand and smiles at him happily.)

20A. Ext. Lakehead University. Day.
(Establishing shot of the university with an identifying sign.)

20B. Int. University Hallway. Day.
(Pete, Lenore, Sadie, Connie and Miss Walker approach a Man in a suit outside the lecture room doors. Pete looks around uncomfortably.)

Miss Walker: *(To Man)* Is this the District Writing Finals?

Man #1: *(Officious)* Yes. They're about to begin.
(Lenore is excited and scared. She hesitates at the door.)

Lenore: I…I don't think…
(Pete puts a hand on her shoulder. She looks up at him.)

Pete: *(Smiling)* Read it to me. Just to me.
(Lenore takes heart in these instructions. She smiles and goes quickly inside followed by the others.)

21. Int. Lecture Hall. Day.
(The lecture hall is quite full of people. A panel of six judges sits at a table at the front listening as Lenore reads her story.)

Lenore: So on that morning before she left, they went by canoe one last time to those favourite places. It was at first light, when the water is a mirror and the trees are still, as if nature is holding her breath.
(Near the front rows sit Miss Walker, Pete, Connie and Sadie listening. Lenore reads directly to her father inspired by his presence. Pete listens intently.)

And there was the beaver and the loon and the hawk circling above the treetops. And below, the trout and the sturgeon slipped silently through the black water.

Creatures as powerful as the great moose, as small as the minnow. She and her father took their place among them.
(Pete, in his solemn features, reveals amazement at his daughter's ability and the touching sentiments of the story.)

And in this world there was a peace and harmony that she knew no matter how far she travelled, she would never find again.

She understood now why her father had brought her here. She felt the morning sun on her face and the gentle rocking of the canoe and smiled because she knew that here would always be her home.
(When Lenore finishes, the hall is silent. Pete, very moved by his daughter's story, rises immediately to his feet. He begins to applaud loudly—the only one in the hall. The Judges look at him with disfavour. But then Sadie applauds and stands and Connie and Miss Walker stand applauding and then others and finally the whole hall is on its feet applauding. Even two of the Judges give polite applause. Connie, Miss Walker and Sadie smile at Pete. Pete looks only at Lenore.

Pete and Lenore, with tears in her eyes, look at each other and smile meaningfully at one another.)

■ Content and Style

1. After you have read the whole screenplay, divide into six groups and discuss one of the three acts in terms of either
   - conflict—what conflicts develop or are resolved in the act?

   OR

   - motivation—why do the characters act the way they do?

   Have each group report on their discussion to the class.

2. In small groups, prepare and perform a scene that you decide is the most dramatic, humorous, or important. Then choose the best performed scene and the best actor in the class, and explain the reasons for your choices.

3. a) Make a glossary of technical terms used in this screenplay, such as *int., ext., frame, stock shot, establishing shot,* and *telephoto lens.*
   b) Draw a storyboard for one of the scenes in this screenplay. Draw a separate picture (with stick figures if you like) for each shot and indicate whether it is a close-up, medium, or long shot.

■ Social Context

4. a) In your notebook, describe how Native lifestyles and values are presented in "Words on a Page" under each of the following headings:
   - making a living
   - the role of men and women
   - the role of dreams
   - home life
   - storytelling
   - the importance of education
   b) With a partner, determine whether Natives are shown in a positive, negative, or stereotypical way. Explain your opinion to the class.

5. a) Copy the following chart in your notebook and fill it in for each scene of the screenplay.

	Who Gains Power?	Who Loses Power?	Whose Power Stays the Same?
Act 1, Scene 1			
Act 1, Scene 2A			
Act 1, Scene 2B			

   b) Use the information in the chart to write a paragraph. Explain how the power people have depends on their position in the family and willingness to change their minds and be flexible.

6. Research one of the topics below and prepare a brief report for the class. You might ask a librarian or another subject teacher to assist you.
   • Thunder Bay and Nipigon: location, population, distance from where you live, methods of travel you could use to get there, and local geography
   • the five most important issues facing Native people today
   • Native spirituality

■ Personal and Imaginative Response

7. In a paragraph, describe your most interesting writing experience.

8. Select the scene from the screenplay you feel would be the hardest to film. Explain why you chose that one.

Being Comfortable With Being "Weird"

BY NAOMI C. POWELL

When you're 12, the last thing you want to be is different. In preteen dialect, "different" is a direct synonym for "weird," and to be weird is to be an outcast. In my elementary school, the weird kids were usually the ones who couldn't afford designer jeans and who failed miserably at sports, often being laughed off the soccer field for their clumsiness.

They usually sat by themselves or with other outcasts, playing quietly or eating their lunches while watching enviously as the "cool" kids scored touchdowns and gave each other high fives. But even for the weird kids, the doors to "coolness" and social acceptance were relatively open: All they had to do was squeeze a new pair of jeans out of their mother and learn how to throw a spiral.

On the other hand, for people like myself, the ultraweird, the doors were not only shut; they were locked so tightly that no amount of Levi's or athletic ability could get them open.

Unlike a lot of other youngsters, I wasn't burdened with a weight problem or unattractive appearance. In fact, I was a rather good-looking kid; I just wasn't interested in being popular. When I hit Grade 7, I was still wearing my older brother's hand-me-down overalls and tennis shoes and had no idea that any world existed outside the one my best friend Lynn and I had created for ourselves. We didn't really have any friends besides each other, but I can't remember ever being lonely or wanting another pal. When I wasn't with Lynn I was perfectly content with my own company, reading, swimming or riding my bike.

In fact, it wasn't until Lynn moved away that I even realized such a treacherous social ladder existed at my school and that, even worse, I was on the bottom rung. All of a sudden I had no one to eat lunch with, to play with or to walk home from school with. I made a few futile attempts to find new friends, but none of the girls were interested in spending time with someone who couldn't care less about shopping or boys or any of the other activities that were of prime importance in Grade 7.

I began to feel like Dorothy in *The Wizard of Oz,* lost in a colourful, complicated world of "cool" kids and "geeks." Unlike Dorothy, I didn't have three good friends to guide me through this social maze; I didn't even have a yellow brick road to tell me if I was going in the right direction.

I spent the next few months in utter misery, begging my mother to let Lynn move in with us or at least to buy me a pair of jeans like the other kids wore. Mom flat out refused to adopt Lynn but did consent to get a few new clothes for me if I would just keep quiet.

With the new jeans I was boosted from ultraweird to just plain weird and was invited to my first Grade 7 party. I dressed with more caution than a bride before her wedding and flounced down the stairs in my new frilly lace skirt and white sweater, determined to find a new best friend.

I had adopted all the cool sayings into my vocabulary, had begun watching TV (something I never had time for in the past),

and had started making beaded necklaces—which I found excruciatingly boring, but everyone else thought it was "rad." While I didn't know the names of more than two kids at school when Lynn was around, I knew everyone now, as well as the kids they hung around with and the ones they hated. My parents had had it up to their eyeballs with this makeup-coated, gum-cracking stranger who kept saying "like" and talked on the phone for hours. I was a walking, talking, teen magazine, and I may have been popular, but I wasn't happy.

The party turned out to be a failure; I spent the entire evening playing basketball in the host's driveway with the boys while the girls looked on with disgust. When I took a break for some punch, I heard one of the "cool" girls whisper to her friend:

"Like, oh my God, she is so weird."

All at once it occurred to me this superficial little wench was right: I was weird. I had tried to be someone I wasn't but couldn't pull it off. I hated "normal" things like makeup, TV and clothes. I wasn't like these girls; I didn't giggle like a three-year-old when a boy spoke to me and I didn't enjoy slathering cosmetics on my face, and I didn't belong at that party.

I left without saying good night, went straight home and scrubbed

my face, fighting desperately with the thick globs of mascara and eye liner that had been eating into my eyes all evening. I ripped the uncomfortable, skin-irritating party clothes from my body and donned my overalls, revelling in their soft denim, so worn it fit every curve of my body like a loose glove. I slipped my feet into my tattered tennis shoes, pulled the laces tight and ran down the stairs to go for a ride on my old 10-speed. I felt a wave of relief roll through my body and decided that even if "weirdness" meant having

no friends at all, I was never going to be that person again. I had to be myself, and for the most part, it was a hell of a lot more fun.

Fortunately, I did make a few friends who were just as weird as I was, and I finished Grade 8 with a smile on my face. But I learned something I've never forgotten and that is to be true to myself. So if there are any parents out there wondering if they're living with their 12-year-old daughter or an explosive preteen night-mare, relax, and have her read this article.

Can't You See?

BY MARIAM KHAN DURRANI

Can't you see
I can't be
what you want
what you please
I can't
wear a mask
I am me, Go away
or accept my way
do I have to raise my voice
to make you understand
I have no choice,
I am what I am…

■ Content and Style

1. a) In your notebook, write any questions you would like to ask
      the narrator of the poem about the reasons for his or her
      feelings.
   b) As a class, discuss whether or not it is important to know
      the answers to your questions in order to enjoy the poem.

2. a) With a partner, make two lists to show how Naomi Powell changes in order to be "cool" and fit in.

Naomi Powell used to...	Then Naomi Powell...

b) Write a paragraph giving your viewpoint on whether the author made the right decision when she decided to stop trying to be cool. Read your paragraph to the class.

■ Social Context

3. a) In two groups, one of only boys and the other of girls, list what it means to be "weird," as well as what it means to be cool.

b) As a class, compare your two lists. Arrive at a conclusion about what qualities are valued by boys and what qualities are valued by girls.

4. With a partner, make a list of some of the different "masks" people wear at different times. Write a story in which the main character has to wear a mask. Share your story with other partnerships.

5. Write a paragraph on something you like about yourself even though others consider it a bit weird
                              OR
write about a time in your life when you wanted to hide something about yourself or wished you were someone else.

■ Personal and Imaginative Response

6. Collect photographs, pictures from magazines, song lyrics, original artwork, and other materials that you feel show what kind of person you are. Make a collage of these. Present your collage to classmates.

7 Form a committee whose task is to bring the school community closer together. Have committee members make a plan to help new people feel accepted. Present your suggestions to your guidance counsellor and ask him or her for feedback.

Ready, Willing and Able

BY RANDY STARKMAN

Jeff Adams had heard every sporting cliche about an athlete having the race of his life, but he was living it. It was a searing 44°C under the noon-day sun in Barcelona, normally *siesta* time, but sleep was hardly on Adams' mind. He was in full flight in the biggest race of his young life, the 1500-metre wheelchair exhibition at the 1992 Summer Olympics. The Brampton, Ontario, athlete had put four years of gut-wrenching workouts into preparing for this moment, for a race that would last just more than three minutes. And it looked like that dedication would pay off handsomely. With just more than 300 metres to go, Adams was just where he wanted to be, in medal contention and ready to strike.

Then it happened. The push ring on his right rear wheel, one of two used to propel the chair, popped right off. Adams watched in complete disbelief as the ring rolled off the track and toward the stands. A wheelchair athlete with one push ring is like a rower with one oar. He was cut adrift.

"As soon as my push ring fell off, I thought, 'That's it. That was my shot. It's over now,'" Adams says.

The push ring disappearing from sight might well have symbolized the Olympic rings slipping from Adams' grasp forever. The International Olympic Committee (IOC) is leaning toward eliminating all demonstration events, cutting off the only avenue that's been available to wheelchair athletes.

There is a bid to get full medal status for some wheelchair events, but that's being dwarfed by a larger, and seemingly futile, attempt to get the IOC to accept 14 separate disabled events at the 1996 Summer Games in Atlanta, Georgia.

Adams doesn't need any reminders that wheelchair athletes aren't taken seriously by big-time international sports officials, but he gets them nevertheless every time he competes in a major event. When he showed up for the Summer Games in Barcelona, they told him he couldn't train on the Olympic track with the other athletes.

"The lady said, 'Can you train on the sidewalk?'" Adams remembers, still incredulous. "Does [Moroccan middle distance star] Said Aouita train on the sidewalks of Barcelona? You can't do it."

Still, left without options, Adams tried to train on the road—for a day, anyway. After nearly getting killed by a car 20 times in the first five minutes, he finally got officials to relent. Still, he wasn't allowed on to the track in peak training hours.

"You've got to push and you've got to shove a little bit," Adams says. "That's what we're a bit unwilling to do. We're politically correct and we don't want to offend anyone."

What Adams is striving for is to have his sport seen as an athletic event, not a disabled event. When a picture of a dejected Adams ran in *The Star* following his Olympic disappointment, several callers complained that wheelchair sport was being portrayed in a bad light. Adams just rolls his eyes when this is mentioned. To him, the picture portrayed just what it should: a gritty competitor trying to deal with defeat.

He says people have this sunny notion of wheelchair sport being a mere pastime for the disabled. He points out that most people, particularly international sports officials, don't realize elite wheelchair athletes are every bit as committed and dedicated as the able-bodied.

Adams, who took a full year off university to concentrate on the final push toward Barcelona, trains twice a day, spending a lot of time in the weight room and on the track.

One of the most frustrating things for Adams is that his Olympic dream is out of his control. The hours he spends honing his talents on the track and in the weight room won't have any influence. The final determination will be made in a posh boardroom somewhere by stodgy sports officials, many of whom have probably never seen his sport live.

Adams doesn't believe there should be events at the Olympics designated only for the disabled. At the last meeting of the Canadian Wheelchair Sport Association, athletes recommended that the able-bodied be allowed to compete in wheelchairs against them. In stating his case for wheelchair events at the Olympics, Adams says it should be a wide-open competition. The wheelchair should just be considered another implement, like a hurdle or javelin.

"It's not a politically acceptable thing for me to say, but people don't realize what the Olympics is," Adams says. "Less than half a per cent of the world's population ever gets to go to the Olympics. Why should you suddenly allow all kinds of people to get in just because they happen to compete in an event where most of the world is excluded?"

Jeff Adams has the Olympic rings tattooed over his heart. He had the artwork emblazoned on his well-muscled chest, interwoven with the maple leaf tattoo he had done in 1989, just one week before the Olympic trials in New Orleans, Louisiana. He did it partly to bolster his confidence about earning a spot in Barcelona, but mostly to symbolize what the whole experience meant to him.

"The Olympics are part of who I am now," he says. "It was my life for at least four years leading up to it. For the last two prior, it was almost all I thought about in terms of my goal."

If the Olympics don't clear a path for wheelchair events, Adams might try a different route. He has toyed with the idea of trying to make the Canadian kayak team. His muscle-to-mass ratio is incredible compared to an average able-bodied person. He discussed the idea with two kayakers in Barcelona.

"If I could ever do that and make it to the Olympics, the question would be over about whether we're athletes," he says. "Hopefully I won't have to do that."

Activities READY, WILLING AND ABLE

■ Content and Style

1. In a group of four, write down Jeff Adams' view of himself. Share what you have written with another group.

2. In order to clearly understand the points in this article, explain to a partner the status wheelchair events had at the Olympics when this article was written. Have your partner explain to you how the article shows that Jeff Adams is "ready, willing and able."

3. In writing, explain the purpose for each of the direct quotations included in this article.

4. Reread the newspaper article to see if the author agrees or disagrees with Jeff Adams. Decide whether or not the author has taken a stand on the issue.

■ Social Context

5. Jeff Adams is concerned that people have a "sunny notion of wheelchair sport being a mere pastime for the disabled." Make a poster that illustrates how he would like the public to view wheelchair athletes.

6. As a class, debate the following resolution: Wheelchair athletes should be able to compete in the regular Olympics.

■ Personal and Imaginative Response

7. Imagine that Jeff Adams competes and wins a medal in the summer Olympics of 2000. As Adams, make a speech to the Canadian press explaining what the medal means to you.

Take Time for 8 Matters of the Heart

BY ED YOUNG

Take time for repose
it is the germ of creation

Take time to read
it is the foundation of wisdom

Take time to think
it is the source of strength

Take time to work
it is the path to patience and success

Take time to play
it is the secret of youth and constancy

Take time to be cheerful
it is the appreciation of life that brings happiness

Take time to share
it is in fellowship and sound relationships
one finds meaning

Take time to rejoice
for joy is the music of the soul.

Im bored !

Activities

■ Content and Style

1. With a partner, explain the connection between the first and second line of each stanza of the poem.

2. List activities you think are important to "take time for." Share your list with a partner and then present the two lists to the class.

■ Social Context

3. Write a character sketch of a person you know who might like to receive this poem as a gift. Explain why you chose this person.

4. Find another poem, prayer, poster, or card with a thoughtful message and bring it to class to read aloud and discuss.

■ Personal and Imaginative Response

5. Write what this poem means to you and where you might post it.

6. Write another stanza for the poem using the words "Take time…" and "it is…." Share your new stanza with classmates.

7. In the original version, the author placed a Chinese character beside each stanza. Write a poem of your own that includes special letters or symbols and share it with classmates.

8. With a partner, decorate this poem with pictures that you think are suitable. Display it for others to view.

1. For one week, as you watch television, make notes on relationships between people in the programs. At the end of the week, choose from your notes

   a) the most positive relationship, and

   b) the most negative relationship.

   For each relationship, write a short description of the people involved. Explain why it is the best example in its category.

2. Prepare an anthology of stories, poems, essays, newspaper or magazine articles, pictures, and drawings that reveal your personality. Include a title page, a dedication page, a table of contents, and an introduction. For each selection in the anthology, write one or two sentences that explain why you included it. Feel free to include your own writing in the anthology.

3. Research information about an older member of your family such as a grandparent. Interview the person about his or her life experiences. Prepare a memory box (container of items of special importance to the person), a scrapbook, or a biography of his or her life. Include items such as the following:

   • photographs or other reminders of the person

   • an account of the person's school life, teenage years, work experience, and other main events

   • lyrics from the person's favourite songs

   • favourite films, radio shows, plays, and/or musicians

4. Choose a scene from the selections in this unit that makes an important statement about relationships. Using "Words on a Page" as a model, create a shooting script for the scene.

5. Imagine that you are a reporter looking for human interest stories. With a partner, examine the relationships in the stories in this unit. Decide which characters you would most like to interview. Make a list of the questions you would like to ask these characters. Then suggest the answers they might give. Compare your work with another pair. In your group of four, decide which three characters you would most like to interview. Write and perform the interview for the class.

Power Tools

STUDENT HANDBOOK

Misused Words

When we communicate with each other, it is important to use words that express our thoughts clearly. The words listed below are ones that are often used incorrectly. As you read the words on each line, see whether you understand the differences between them. If you are not sure of the differences in their meanings, use a dictionary or talk with a partner or your teacher to find out. For your own writing assignments, keep a list of words that you have not used correctly. The list will be helpful to you for future writing assignments.

a lot, allot
accept, except
advise, advice
affect, effect
all ready, already
all together, altogether
knew, new
know, no
loose, lose
quite, quiet
than, then
their, they're, there
to, too, two
where, we're, wear, were
your, you're

Common Sentence Errors

By the time you are in Grade 9, you should be writing correct sentences and paragraphs. A sample of common sentence errors follows. In your notebook, you can keep another list of mistakes that you and your classmates often make.

Comma Splice

Example: I liked the story by Monica Hughes, it deals with important issues in our society.

What's wrong? There are two good sentences here, but the punctuation is wrong. After each complete thought, you need a period. A comma cannot be used between two sentences.

How to fix it: I liked the story by Monica Hughes. It deals with important issues in our society.

Run-On Sentence

Example: I got a lot of work done today I finished the reading and I went to the library and I started my assignment but I didn't fill in the chart because I couldn't find it.

What's wrong? There are too many thoughts loosely connected in one sentence. They are strung together with *and's* and *but's*.

How to fix it: I got a lot of work done today. I finished the reading and I went to the library. I started my assignment but I didn't fill in the chart because I couldn't find it.

Sentence Fragment

Example: Because I like having my homework done on time. The narrator thinking about the loss of his friend.

What's wrong? The information in these sentences is not in the form of a complete thought.

How to fix it: Because I like having my homework done on time, I do it as soon as I go home.
The narrator is thinking about the loss of his friend.

Paragraphs

A paragraph is a group of sentences about the same idea or topic. The main idea of the paragraph is expressed in a topic sentence. The rest of the sentences in the paragraph develop the topic. There are different kinds of paragraphs. The two types that you will most often be asked to write are narrative and expository.

Narrative

A narrative presents a series of events that tell a story. Short stories are made up of narrative paragraphs. A new narrative paragraph begins when there is a change in time, place, activity, or speaker.

Expository

An exposition is used to inform, clarify, define, explain, or analyse. Expository paragraphs are used in essays, reports, and research papers. A new expository paragraph begins when a new point in the explanation or argument is made.

Tips on Research

When we need more information on a topic, we do research. There are a number of steps you need to take as you do your research. Begin by focussing on what your topic is, what you already know about the topic, and what you need to find out. Then, you should think about where you might get the information you need. There are many sources of information depending on the topic.

Research Tools

- resource centre
- print sources (magazines, books, newspapers)
- computer (data bases, bibliographies, electronic encyclopedias)
- people (personal experience, experts, interviews, surveys)
- non-print media (film, television, video, slides, artwork, photographs)

Gathering Information

When gathering information from any of these sources, you should
- reread or review materials slowly and carefully,
- be selective,
- keep notes from the source, and
- record the name of the source.

Presenting Information

After you have gathered the information, you should decide how to prepare and present it. You might want to create a written or oral report, a dramatization or documentary, a bulletin board display or a cartoon. After completing your presentation, you should think about the experience. Decide what went well and what didn't go well. Think about what you might do differently the next time you do research.

Tips on Interviewing

Before you interview someone, you must take time to get ready. Start by listening to interviews on the news and other broadcasts on radio and television. You might also read interviews in magazines. Then, complete the following steps:
- Decide what it is you want to find out. Write down questions that will lead you to the information you want.
- Start with basic fact questions: who? what? when? where? why? and how? Avoid questions that will produce only "yes" or "no" answers.
- Set up your interview by phoning or writing the person you wish to interview. Always be polite, speak clearly, and agree to meet at a place and time that is good for him or her.
- Take your questions, a pen or pencil (and a backup), and a notebook to the interview. You may also wish to take along a tape recorder to record the interview. Remember to check with the interviewee before recording the conversation.
- Thank your interviewee when the interview is over. Follow up with a thank-you note a few days later.

Tips on the Writing Process

Prewriting
- Pick a topic that interests you and allows you to display your knowledge and writing skills.
- Discuss and brainstorm ideas about the topic with classmates and your teacher.
- Gather any information you need from the sources listed in *Research Tools.*
- Group together similar ideas.
- Decide what information to keep and what to drop.
- Make an outline of the ideas.

Drafting
- Write the drafts of your project.
- If you use a word processor, make a printout of each draft.

Revising
Alone or with a partner, decide on changes you could make using the following questions as guidelines:
- Reorder: Are the ideas in the best order?
- Add: Have you included all the information you need? Have you used examples to explain your ideas? Does your introduction make people want to read on?
- Delete: Have you dropped information you don't need?
- Change: Is there a better way to explain your points?

Editing
Be sure to check the following:
- punctuation
- spelling and capitalization (If you are using a word processor, remember your spell checker.)
- grammar
- sentence variety (Use sentences of different lengths and types.)
- clarity

Finishing
Complete the following:
- Create a cover page.
- Create a final copy to hand in.
- Add the rough drafts.
- Include research notes.
- Add the assignment sheet.

Tips on Oral Activities and Presentations

Improvisation/Role Playing/Dramatization
When people watch you perform an improvisation, role play, or dramatization, they should be able to understand the story you are presenting. As you prepare a presentation for an audience, follow these guidelines:
- Practise the performance until you feel comfortable with it.
- Know your material well enough to avoid reading.
- Speak slowly, loudly, and clearly, and in a tone you think the character would use.
- Use simple props, costumes, and sound effects to help set the mood.
- Be sure all props and costumes are ready before the day of the presentation.
- Be sure the audience can see and hear everything.
- Use movements that help show character and keep the audience's interest.

Debating
A debate is an organized argument between two teams. The focus of the debate is a sentence called the resolution. The resolution is stated in the affirmative. For example:
- Correct: Comic books are dangerous because they offer unrealistic ways to escape from the difficult problems of the world.
- Incorrect: Comic books are *not* dangerous because they offer unrealistic ways to escape from the difficult problems of the world.

The team that supports the resolution is the affirmative side. The team that does not support the resolution is the negative side. Following are some guidelines for having a formal debate.

- The **chair** introduces the topic and the speakers, sets out the time limits, and states the judges' decisions. It is up to the chair to keep order.
- The **timekeeper** makes sure that the speakers keep to the time allowed and warns them when their time is up.
- The **judges** might include several students and possibly a teacher or guest. They should think about how effective and clear the speakers' arguments are when deciding which team is more convincing.

- The **first affirmative speaker** has four minutes to introduce the topic, state all the affirmative points, and prove the point that is the focus.
- The **first negative speaker** has four minutes to state the arguments for the negative side, and prove the arguments of the first speaker are incorrect.
- The **second affirmative speaker** has three minutes to prove the arguments of the previous speaker are incorrect, and state own arguments and proof.
- The **second negative speaker** has three minutes to prove any outstanding arguments are incorrect, state own arguments and proof, and make a summary of the arguments for the negative side.
- The **first affirmative speaker** has one minute to prove arguments already made are incorrect and make a summary of the affirmative arguments.

Speeches and Reports to the Class
- Research the topic and write your speech or report using guidelines under *Research, Writing Process,* and *Dramatization.*
- Try to keep eye contact with the audience.
- Use movements that feel natural and are not distracting.

Presentations
- Group presentations should focus on the skills and talents of every member.
- Practice is important for good presentations.
- Use audio-visual aids. Rehearse with them in the space where the presentation will take place.
- Be sure all props, costumes, and audio-visual aids are ready before the presentation.
- Keep people in the audience interested by asking them questions, or giving them a mini-quiz or a survey.

Tips on Working With a Partner or Group

Working with your classmates will help you to become more flexible and willing to listen to and be accepting of their ideas and opinions. However, it takes time to develop skills that will help you work well with other people. The following lists identify helpful and unhelpful group activity behaviour. These lists can help you improve your skills and also evaluate yourself as a partner or group member.

Helpful Behaviour

1. Beginning the Group Activity
- getting down to work quickly
- setting goals
- sharing the work

2. Working Together
- staying on topic
- listening carefully to each other
- respecting viewpoints that differ from your own
- giving your opinions and ideas

- helping to make decisions
- discussing ideas thoroughly

- trying to resolve differences

3. Finishing the Group Activity
- co-operating with each other
- completing the task
- thanking people for the work they did

Unhelpful Behaviour

1. Beginning the Group Activity
- wasting time
- being unfocussed
- not doing your share

2. Working Together
- going off topic
- interrupting or ignoring others
- putting down viewpoints that differ from your own
- not getting involved in the process
- fence-sitting
- discussing ideas in a shallow way
- arguing

3. Finishing the Group Activity
- controlling others
- disrupting the process
- criticizing people for the work they did

Tips on Media

Film/Video

A good way to begin working with film or video is to notice how scenes are shot as you watch television shows. Pay attention to how long the shots are, what sound effects are used, and where the characters are standing. Whatever equipment you use, you should follow these steps:

- Unless you are filming something like an interview, create a storyboard and/or a script.
- Decide who will be the camera operator, director, lighting person, sound technician, and so on.
- Rehearse before you begin shooting.
- Make sure the camera is loaded and set correctly, and that there is enough light and as little background noise as possible.
- Use a tripod to keep the camera as steady as possible or brace your elbows against your body while holding the camera.
- Choose the opening shot carefully because it tells the viewer where the action is taking place, what time of day it is, and so on.
- Try to vary the distance of your shots to provide a variety of close-ups, medium shots, and long shots.

Storyboards

A storyboard is a series of drawings that show the content, type, and order of the camera shots in a film or video, as well as the audio (dialogue and sound effects) for each shot. While storyboards are used mostly for television advertisements, you can also use them for scenes from poems or short stories, or for planning scenes from scripts. The following tips should help you create a storyboard:

- The frames or shots can range from rough sketches to colour pictures.
- Draw the shots as if you are looking through the lens of a camera.
- You don't always need to include dialogue.

Visual Literacy

Some of the visuals you will be asked to create are the following:

• collage
• poster
• advertisement
• book cover
• illustration
• title page

As you prepare these visuals, keep in mind the following:

• Be original.
• Make a design that will lead the viewer's eyes to an interesting focal point.
• The visuals should focus on the message, emotion, or idea you wish to present.
• Talk to your visual arts teacher about ideas of design.

Collage

A collage is a visual design of paper, cloth, photographs, or other material stuck to a background. A collage should make a statement about an idea or a theme. The following tips should help you when making a collage:

• Think about what you want to say.
• Decide what materials to use: photographs, your own words and drawings, fabric, ticket stubs, shells, buttons, string, and so on.
• Decide what background to use. You don't have to put it on paper. You could use fabric, maps, boxes, plastic containers, or tin cans.
• After you have collected the materials, try out different ways to arrange the pieces before you stick them to the background.
• Attach the pieces to the background and display your collage for others to see.

Glossary

analogy: a comparison that focusses on something similar between two things that are otherwise not the same

anthology: a collection of material linked by theme. This material usually includes poems, short stories, plays, or non-fiction selections, or a combination of these by one author or a number of authors.

author: a person who writes short stories, novels, non-fiction selections, or other material

autobiography: material written by a person about his or her own life

biographical information: material about a person's life such as birth date, education, and career

biography: material written by someone about another person's life

CD-ROM: an acronym for a "Compact **D**isk **R**ead-**O**nly Memory." This means that data can be stored on the disk and retrieved, but not changed. Often libraries have dictionaries, encyclopedias, and data bases for various subjects on CD-ROM.

conflict: a struggle between individuals or forces, for instance, the protagonist in a short story and someone or something else. Most conflicts can be described as one of the following: an individual versus him- or herself, an individual versus others, an individual versus the environment, an individual versus cosmic forces, or an individual versus technology.

dialogue: a conversation between two or more people. A dialogue can take the form of a script or a narrative. In a narrative, quotation marks must be used for direct speech.

diary: a person's private record of his or her feelings and experiences

dramatic reading: the reading out loud of a selection to bring life and meaning to it. Often it includes the use of props, costumes, lighting, and movement.

dramatization: a performance that may be based on or stem from a selection

essay: a piece of non-fiction writing that focusses on a single idea and includes an introduction, body, and conclusion

fable: a story meant to teach a lesson. It often focusses on human weaknesses and includes talking animals.

glossary: a list of special, technical, or difficult words with definitions or comments

imagery: the pattern of images, or word pictures, in a single piece of writing

images: word pictures used to explain an idea, strengthen a feeling, reveal character, or create mood. Images are most frequently found in poetry, but appear in all types of writing.

improvisation: performance without a script. It usually involves the performance of dialogue and action invented spontaneously.

journal: a place for writing opinions, thoughts, and feelings

learning log: a place to record information about a particular topic

metaphor: an implied comparison between two unlike things that speaks of one thing as if it were the other (In "Dave's Fall," page 7, the first line is a metaphor: "In fall I see stained glass sky....")

monologue: a long speech by one person; a scene or short play for one actor; a part of a play in which a single actor speaks alone

mood: the feeling created by a piece of writing. It is made up of many things, including setting, characterization, diction, and imagery.

narration: the telling in detail of an event or series of events

narrator: a person who tells a story

periodical index: a listing in book form or on CD-ROM of articles in magazines, journals, and newspapers. The index is arranged alphabetically under subject headings and author surnames.

personal response: a reaction to something you see or hear that expresses your feelings and thoughts about it

photo essay: a series of photographs, sometimes including words, used to explain an idea

plot: the series of actions or events that make up a short story, play, poem, or other narrative writing. It usually centres on a conflict.

point-form outline: an outline of the main ideas of a piece of writing, such as an essay or report, written in the fewest words possible

point of view: the perspective from which a short story or piece of writing is seen or told. In first-person point of view, the story is told from the point of view of the narrator, who uses the pronouns *I* or *we.* In third-person point of view, the story is told using the pronouns *he, she, it,* or *they.* The narrator can know what is happening in more than one place and what more than one character is thinking at any time.

prototype: the original or model for something

role play: to pretend that you are another person by trying to think, act, speak, and react exactly the way the person would

satire: a work making fun of human behaviour, usually to cause laughter, thought, and change

scrapbook: a book in which pictures, photographs, or clippings are kept

screenplay: a story or play written for production as a motion picture or television program, including a description of characters, scenes, and dialogue

script: the format for writing a play, whether it is presented on stage, radio, television, or as a movie. It usually begins with a list of the characters and is followed by all the lines spoken by the actors, in order, and stage directions, which describe what the stage should look like, what special effects should be used, and how the actors should speak and move.

simile: a comparison between two unlike things using *like* or *as* to make the comparison (In "Dave's Fall," page 7, the second and third lines are a simile: "and elm trees like arches/in an abandoned cathedral….")

sound collage: a variety of sounds on audio tape, possibly with spoken words, to explain an idea, mood, or theme

stanza: a group of lines of poetry printed together and joined by thought, metre, rhyme, or all of these

stereotype: a standard or stock image of a group of people in which a few symbols are selected from a large number of possibilities to represent the group

style: the individual way an author expresses him- or herself. It is created by such things as sentences, diction, and images.

summary: a brief outline of the main ideas of a paragraph or a longer piece of writing

symbol: something concrete used to represent an abstract idea (A dove is a symbol of peace.)

theme: the central idea of a piece of writing, usually implied rather than directly stated

thesis: a single idea that expresses a writer's attitude towards the subject of an essay

thumbnail sketch: a small sketch that shows what a final product might look like

vertical files: resource material in libraries collected from newspapers, magazines, and other sources, and stored in file folders arranged by subject and/or people's names

YOUR

ENVIRONMENTS

No Place for Teenagers

BY MARIA BOHUSLAWSKY

The suburban dream is about owning a home and raising your children in a safe place with a big yard.

But it was never clear exactly how teenagers fit into the picture. Today, teens are saying there's no place for them in the suburbs. The result is boredom. ← Ennuyent

One of the most dramatic examples occurred early one recent Sunday morning in suburban Kanata near Ottawa when scores of teens rampaged through a shopping area after a bush party attended by 2000. They vandalized cars, destroyed bikes, uprooted street lamps, broke into stores and set garbage cans on fire.

"There's lots to do for little kids but nothing for us," says Nadeen Gelowsky, 18, of Kanata, who attended the party but left before the vandalism. "There's no place for a teen to let off some steam."

Ottawa architect Philip Piazza, an expert on environmental psychology, says the teens are right.

Suburbs lead to a feeling of alienation because there's not much except houses. Everything is too far apart and geared towards cars, while teens are on foot.

"This isn't a policing situation or a parental problem," Piazza says. "This is a basic planning problem. Everyday human needs are not being met."

Piazza says 500 metres is considered walking distance. But in the suburbs few facilities are within walking distance.

"If the only place to meet is in a mall, which is strictly geared to material values, what values are teens exploring? What adventures do they have?"

Even going to their schoolyard to toss a ball with friends is difficult, he notes, when most kids are bused to school. "Teens feel alienated when they have no access to facilities. There's no question that vandalism is one of the results."

Gelowsky says the type of destruction in Kanata occurs daily but on a much smaller level: "Some people feel they have to rebel. They have to show that there's nothing to do and that they want something."

Gelowsky says teens end up hanging out at the mall or wandering around in packs. Or they go to Ottawa or Hull. She and her friends often go to Ottawa where they enjoy sightseeing, bowling, walking around the Byward Market and attending spectator sports.

While one of the attractions of suburbia is parks, Gelowsky says those are not really available to teens.

The ball diamonds are rented by leagues and teenagers have to watch out for youngsters on playground equipment. If they go to schoolyards they are chased away by janitors because they are tearing up the grass or might break a window.

Ben Gianni, head of the School of Architecture at Carleton University, says one of the problems is that there are few public places in suburbs. Even the mall is private and teens can be ordered to leave.

"You're completely jailed in a way. You have a tremendous amount of energy in adolescence, and there's no place to go. You can't walk any more so you're stuck in the house at each other's throats."

Piazzas and squares are no longer used because they don't accommodate cars, says Gianni. Someone should take another look at them, with pedestrians in mind, he says.

Philip Cowell, 14, of Kanata, says teens don't feel they have a place of their own. "Teens enjoy walking around a mall looking at things. But a lot of people in Kanata think teens are bad. We get shooed away a lot."

He says security guards in malls tell teens to leave, as do staff at the local doughnut shop. "We're not allowed to sit in there unless we buy something."

A new arcade with sports games is geared toward youth. While Cowell says he enjoys it, it's not something he does more than once every three weeks.

Fran Klodawsky, who teaches urban geography at Carleton University, says that in the suburbs there just aren't the variety of options as in the city and things aren't as close together.

For example, in central Ottawa there are free outdoor concerts, museums, art galleries and an interesting street life.

Another advantage of the city is anonymity, which gives adolescents the freedom to explore. "A teenager might be willing to wander around an art gallery if they think nobody will see them or tell their parents," Klodawsky says.

Cowell agrees that teens need to spread their wings without being watched. "Wherever I go, my mom's friends stop me and talk to me. It gets tiresome."

Ryan Blais, 14, who lives in nearby Barrhaven, says there is nothing in his suburb besides a sports centre. "I feel left out of most stuff. I have friends who live downtown and they do all kinds of stuff. I'm bored most of the time."

Blais says it takes at least an hour and two buses to get outside of Barrhaven.

"You're basically on the bus all the time," says Lara Wigmore, 14, also of Barrhaven. "I feel really far from everything. I'd go out more, but it takes so long. It takes too much effort. You have to really plan it."

And depending on the hour, she may end up having to walk a mile [1.6 km] home at night from the bus stop.

As a result she says she watches a lot of TV. And she is very happy that her parents have decided to move, prompted by the needs of her older sister who is going to Carleton.

Barry Wellar, who teaches urban planning at the University of Ottawa, says he doesn't believe the suburbs work for anybody. "It's very difficult to create a sense of community if your objective is to get out of it simply because there's nothing there."

He says if teens in Kanata are unhappy, they're likely reflecting the unhappiness of their parents.

It's a high-tech community and

many of the adults work in competitive, high stress jobs. Well-educated and well-placed, they have high expectations about what material goods they should have, says Wellar.

"You pay a price for living in the fast track."

Gelowsky says it would be nice if there were ball diamonds that were available at night just to play catch or get some friends together for a softball game. Other ideas include a bowling alley and a non-alcoholic dance club.

She thinks that in the long run these types of facilities would save money on vandalism.

But her friend Laurie Seguin says it's important to consult teens. "Sometimes the city tries to do something and teens think it's stupid."

Orleans is a suburban community that consulted its teens. One of the results is the Orleans Youth Centre.

Set in an old legion hall, it has a small gym, pool table, weight equipment, shuffleboard tables, ping-pong, a TV for movie nights and a small canteen. It is successful, with more than 250 members.

"When they're bored and frustrated, that leads to problems," says manager Dan Rees. "The suburbs look like an enemy to them. They get into vandalism and other forms of bad behavior. The more

choices they have, the more opportunity they have to make good ones."

Andrea Beaumier, 14, says Orleans meets her needs and those of her friends.

"We go to the pool hall, the arcade, the movie theatre and the mall. We just want a place to hang around...and talk. Someplace where our parents aren't."

Piazza says one answer to suburban teen boredom is to build up existing communities. Adolescents should be involved in the development of new communities and their input should be seriously considered.

It's time the malls gave something back to the community, he says. One way is to provide facilities that interest youth.

Piazza suggests that communities consider setting up a non-bureaucratic storefront office to facilitate kids' activities—a place to set up their own dances, organize camping and ski trips or football leagues.

Yvan Roy, supervisor of the Youth Services Bureau in Orleans, agrees teens need a meeting place. He says some 30 to 40 teens a day drop into the bureau at the Place D'Orleans shopping centre to sit and talk.

"You don't have to make it complicated. They just need the space. They need to be with each other."

■ Content and Style

1. With a partner, list the major problems that the author says teen-agers have in suburban communities. Determine whether or not you agree with the author. Explain to classmates your response to the problems you listed.

2. With a partner, decide whether or not there is enough evidence in the article to convince the reader that the needs of teens who live in the suburbs are being overlooked. Name other groups who could have been asked for their views.

■ Social Context

3. As a class, brainstorm ideas that would help suburban communities meet the needs of teenagers. Choose the best ideas. Then write a report to your local government representative to suggest ways to meet teen needs in future suburban developments.

■ Personal and Imaginative Response

4. Select a suburb you are familiar with and imagine that you are a tour guide. Consider the following:
   - places you would stop at for visitors to explore
   - comments you would make about the homes, places of business, special features
   - services the community offers

   Write a dialogue for the tour. Have classmates help you perform it.

The Essential Mallmanac

BY PHIL PATTON

You know someone—we all know someone—who belongs to the school of the Calculated Casual Dress. The outfit looks just thrown on, but in fact, hours of study have gone into it—the faded jeans torn just so at the knees, the tossed-on sweater that actually took forty-five minutes of painstaking arrangement.

The same thing is true of the shopping mall. While everything seems to be just randomly there, there are highly developed theories behind why everything is exactly the way it is. We go there on impulse, walk into stores on impulse—nearly half of all our purchases, experts say, are made that way. But while we enjoy the illusion of free will in the mall, a whole industry has evolved to calculate the consequences of those casual impulses we have.

In its four decades of existence, the mall has grown from a novelty into an institution, as much a center of our daily lives as Main Street

was in times past. If aliens from a distant galaxy wanted to understand North Americans, and especially North American teenagers, they could do no better than to land their spaceship in a mall. But to understand how the mall got there in the first place, where it came from, and why we love it, they'd have to travel back into history and go behind the scenes—into the minds of the mall's creators.

We tend to think of malls as monolithic department stores, record shops, earring pagodas, and nerds who never leave the video arcade. But the people who run malls think of them in terms of square feet—and how much money they can make from each foot.

Ever wonder why there are so many shoe stores? The people who run malls know why. They know it's because the average woman buys six pairs of shoes a year, and younger women more than that.

And since shoes are relatively small items, lots of them will fit into a store's square feet. Mall owners also know that each of us will stay an average of an hour and twenty minutes each time we visit the mall; that most shoppers come by car; that fifteen- to nineteen-year-olds spend an average of $25.96 each trip; and that 86 percent of us will buy something at the "food court" while we're there. They know that teenagers visit an average of 3.5 stores per trip—and that malls earn about three hundred billion dollars each year.

Mall owners watch over their tenants, too, and often have final say over a store's decor, the height of its display counters, and even what kind of rock and roll a place can blast. They decide when stores will open, when they'll close, and how much each one has to kick in for Christmas decorations. They determine which stores go where in the mall; a women's store, for example, is likely to have a men's store nearby so couples can shop together. Mall owners spend a lot of time and effort figuring out stuff like this. If it's there, you can bet it's there for a reason.

What's not there isn't there for a reason, too. Like windows. Most malls don't have windows. Sure they have skylights, but there's nothing else to give you a glimpse of the world outside. The absence of windows keeps your attention inside, on the stores. It also gives the mall much of its spaceship feeling—that very vast and confusing spaceship feeling.

There are always the maps to help you find your way: black polygons with red numbers and arrows that say, "You are here." But by the time you figure out exactly where "here" is and boldly set off—to Baskin-Robbins, let's say—you get fifty feet [15 m] away and realize you're lost. So you walk into The Gap or Foot Locker, forgetting about the ice cream and ending up with jeans and sneakers instead. That's not exactly a coincidence.

There's a mall principle called Reilly's Law of Retail Gravitation, which basically means that the huge department stores, or "anchors," are there to lure you to the mall—and that two or more anchors will lure you through the mall and past all the shops. Besides, "people don't walk in straight lines," says shopping-center designer Jon Jerdé, whose job it is to keep it that way. (Malls are, above all, for walking—a point confirmed by the "mall walking" fitness clubs that have sprung up across the continent.) You will, needless to way, eventually find what you want, but only after you've walked past lots of other things you weren't aware you wanted until you passed them.

Of course, once you've found all the stuff you didn't know you wanted until you found it, you've got to go out and find your car. Nowhere is the science of mall planning more evident than in the parking lot. Mall-management experts will tell you that parking density approaches 100 percent at about 2:00 p.m. on a Saturday afternoon (but you knew that) and that the smaller cars of the eighties mean that parking spaces can be reduced from the previous 9 feet by 20 feet [2.5 m by 6.1 m] to 8 feet by 17.5 feet [2.4 m by 5.3 m]. If a mall's just starting out, though, the spaces will be painted a foot [30.5 cm] wider than usual so that the parking lot will look full and people driving by will wonder what they're missing.

The word *mall* is a good, solid old English word that originally meant a strip of green lawn where a croquetlike game called pall-mall was played. But for forty years now mall has meant just one thing to most of us: a covered shopping center. The birth of the modern mall can be dated exactly: October 8, 1956, when Southdale Center in Edina, Minnesota, opened its doors.

There was a very good reason why the first mall was in Minnesota: surveys showed that with only 126 days of "ideal" weather in the state each year, an open-air mall could go broke. The covered mall, kept constantly at 68°F [20°C], gave store owners 365 days of good weather. "In Southdale Center," the ads promised, "every day will be a perfect shopping day!" The same formula answered the hotter problems of the Sun Belt, and the mall became the perfect shopping mode for Phoenix and Miami as well as Buffalo and Boston.

A major factor in the development of the mall was the creation of the Interstate Highway System in 1956. Just before Southdale opened, belts of highways were thrown around most American cities; it was on those belts that the malls found themselves at home. And it was there that they grew, on the outskirts of cities—lording over and often destroying the economies of the old downtowns.

The early mall were aimed at traditional homemaker moms. "You and Junior drive a few blocks to the Southdale Center," the ads trumpeted, "park on the lower level...walk in, and you're enjoying June in January!" To mall developers in the fifties and sixties, the very mention of the word *teenager* inspired visions of black leather jackets, switchblades, and used cars lacking mufflers—not what they were eager to attract. Some mall owners even limited the number of eating places they'd allow, figuring the hungry kids would go home to eat. Truth is, they were afraid of them. They didn't know just where teenagers fit into the orderly world of the mall.

And then, as they always do, mall planners did some studies and discovered what was really going on. They found out that some kids were spending several hours a day in the mall, seeing and being seen, meeting their friends, hanging out. They realized that the mall was in many ways an extension of the halls at school. They realized that these kids were *shopping*. Teenagers had money—a lot more money, in fact, than kids did when malls were first built. And they found out that no one was called Junior anymore.

So mall owners put in video arcades and welcomed fast-food outlets. They brought in movie theaters and began to run mall-wide promotions tied in with popular teen movies. (Today half of all movie theaters are located in malls or shopping centers.) They loaded up the place with shoe stores. And the golden age of the mall rat was born.

With all this mall science, you'd think that malls everywhere would end up the same. But the best malls really reflect their location and clientele.

Atlanta is a big mall city, with nearly forty of them on the interstates that line its perimeter. They've become Atlanta's real Main Street—and the pace and tone and manners you encounter in the malls support every cliché you've ever heard about southern hospitality and politeness.

And there's the Houston Galleria, which boasts an ice-skating rink (a triumph over the hot climate and steamy landscape of the city's tract houses.) The mall owners even run a summer camp for kids—Camp Galleria.

The malls of Los Angeles range from the giant Del Amo Fashion Center, in suburban Torrance, which is said to be larger than the state of Monaco and even has its own credit card, to Sherman Oaks Galleria, immortalized in *Fast Times at Ridgemont High* and *Valley Girl*.

Of course, malls tend to have more in common with each other than not, in part because of the subindustries that support them—from the omnipresent "Pitch In" trash receptacles manufactured in St. Louis to the outfit that specializes in supplying Santa Clauses for the malls—Western Temporary Services, which promises that its Santas are carefully trained at its own University of Santa Claus.

Some malls have grown so huge that they're cities in themselves. The largest of them all is the West Edmonton Mall in Edmonton, Alberta, which has an ice-skating rink, an amusement park, the world's largest wave pool, a covered lagoon with four submarines, and some 828 specialty shops in addition to its four anchors. And one hot topic of mall people's lips is the condo mall—you live right where you shop.

The look of malls is changing, too. The new generation of malls has taken on the shapes and colors of the post-modern architectural look—Miami Vice colors applied to classical columns and pediments and arches. But the next wave is also taking its cue from the past. San Diego's Horton Plaza, designed by Jon Jerdé, represents a return to the European styles that inspired Southdale's architect, Austrian Victor Gruen, as well as the wave of "festival marketplaces" now sweeping the country. Like Harborplace, in Baltimore, and New Market Mall, in Columbus, Ohio, these malls are putting villa-type shopping back in urban downtowns: with lots of open-air shops, they're like Italian hill towns, bustling with pushcarts, jugglers, cafés, and popcorn vendors. They offer "a sense of life," says Jerdé, "an urban adventure rather than the usual neat little packages of suburban malls."

At the 1985 opening of Horton Plaza, a high-wire walker crossed the plaza without a net, hundreds of pastel balloons were released, confetti was strewn everywhere, and colorful smoke shells were shot from cannons. It was a scene meant to recall the bazaars of Morocco, a Greek island village, the town square of yesteryear. It was all very casual...and all very calculated.

Activities   THE ESSENTIAL MALLMANAC

■ Content and Style

1. With a partner, reread the article and list the good and bad features of malls.

2. In chart form, list the main points made in "The Essential Mallmanac" and "No Place for Teenagers." Show on your chart which points are similar and which are unique to each article.

■ Social Context

3. In a group of three, decide how the structure and atmosphere of a mall affects the behaviour of people shopping there. (If you haven't thought about this before, visit a mall and, equipped with a notebook, observe the layout of the mall, the sounds in the mall, and what activities people are doing.) Share your observations and conclusions with the class.

4. Research other articles about malls using the periodical index and/or other reference material in your library. Consider the following:
   • types of malls
   • sizes of malls
   • special features of malls
   • predictions writers are making about malls of the future

   Use your research to prepare a report for the class.

■ Personal and Imaginative Response

5. Take the point of view of a person unfamiliar with suburban life who has just spent an afternoon in a shopping mall. Write a diary entry in which she or he reflects on this experience.

6. In a small group, decide what questions you would like to have answered about malls. Arrange to interview the manager of a mall, as well as shop managers, salespeople, and a range of customers from teens to seniors. You might record your interviews on audio cassette or video, but ask permission from the management first. Present your findings to the class.

7. The mall setting has inspired scenes in films, television shows, and novels. In groups, brainstorm how the mall could serve as the setting for a short story, poem, video, or some other creative piece. Each group member should choose one of the ideas and develop it into a finished work for presentation to the class.

8. List features not usually found in malls that you would include in a design of an ideal shopping plaza. Make a floor plan of your mall and be prepared to sell the rest of the class on your design.

Interview With Victor Malarek

BY ANDREA MOZAROWSKI

Victor Malarek, a former street kid, has become an advocate for kids who have no one to speak out for them. Born in La Chine, Quebec, in 1948, he was placed in a boys home at the age of ten along with his two brothers when his parents separated and the welfare authorities refused to let them stay with their mother. He suffered humiliation and violence at the hands of both staff and other children. Returning home years later, he took to the streets to avoid his alcoholic, abusive father. When he was 17 he was arrested for armed robbery and placed in a detention centre. A lenient judge gave him a break and he began to turn his life around. He started as an office boy at *Weekend Magazine* and later landed a job as a police reporter with the *Montreal Star* newspaper. That led him to university at night and a career in journalism. He wrote for *The Globe and Mail* newspaper, often focussing on abandoned children and the child welfare system. In 1984 his autobiography *Hey Malarek!: The True Story of a Street Kid Who Made It* was published. Later he wrote *Merchants of Misery: Inside Canada's Illegal Drug Scene* and *Haven's Gate: Canada's Immigration Fiasco.* He now works as a host of *The 5th Estate,* an investigative current affairs television show.

Andrea: If you try to remember yourself as a child before you went to the boys home, what would you say your needs were?

Victor: To know that I was really loved and cared for by my parents. That I could walk around the house and not feel threatened or afraid that when my father would come home, the whole place would turn upside down with his violent behaviour if he was drunk. Feeling safe, feeling secure, feeling loved.

Andrea: How did you end up on the streets?

Victor: Eventually we came out of the boys home. My father, while we were in the boys home, had gone to a penitentiary. He got cancer while he was in the penitentiary and they let him out early. The situation at home was really, really bad, very tense. Most of the time I would stay away from home as often as I possibly could, which meant basically hanging around the streets and not having to see a situation which was completely driving me insane. And so I would go to the streets and there I would find my own strange solace.

Andrea: What was the hard part of that existence?

Victor: You know, really there wasn't that much of a hard part. The hard part was going home. I didn't give a damn if I slept out under a balcony or a set of stairs that led up to somebody's house. It didn't matter to me and that was better than having to go home and face the reality of a dying father who was abusing drugs and abusing alcohol.

Andrea: Your street sounds a lot better than I imagine the street the kids now find. So if a kid goes out onto the street today, what is he or she going to find?

Victor: When a kid goes to the streets, he's gonna find himself very much alone and very much isolated. But there's a whole subculture out there waiting for him.

It's a specific group of people who will take him up and make him part of this incredibly bizarre family on the streets. These are people who are going to want to use these kids. They're out there all the time and they can pick the runaway out of a crowd of 10 000 people because they look lost and often they think they're on some kind of adventure. There's a hard core out there that are extremely dangerous and do this on a regular basis. And you can't escape them. You're going to owe them in the end; that's the reality in the end for these kids. And you're going to owe them big time.

Andrea: Is there any way to resist these people or keep to yourself?

Victor: If you had the strength and the wherewithal to resist these people, you wouldn't run to the streets.

Now, on the other side of the coin, there are organizations and people who are out there looking for kids who look lost and who may be being abused by that subculture. But what they have to cut through and where it's really difficult to reach these kids is this incredible fear these kids have.

Today the kids are running away as an incredible escape. A lot of them are very sad children who are running, very battered children. Most of the kids I knew who were running in the sixties didn't like curfews and they didn't like the school control. Now these kids who run don't know what they're running to and when they find out it's usually too late. And the sad reality is that very, very few street kids ever get out of the streets. And those who go in at 14, 15, and 13, I would say probably 50 per cent or more are dead before they're 25.

Andrea: What advice would you give a kid who is contemplating running away or is already living on the streets?

Victor: You've got to find somebody. The one thing I was missing in my time was I didn't have an adult to go to. I had no adult friend. Today, if you can, find someone, a social worker, a teacher to confide in, that kind of thing.

Andrea: So, you would say look for someone you can talk to?

Victor: Yeah. You got to look for somebody you can talk to. The damn thing that's really hard, though, is finding trust. But I think for teenagers, they probably could find a friend easier in school than anywhere else. And it would be in a teacher. And that's what they would look for unless they attend a church or a synagogue or some kind of temple and they can reach out to someone spiritually. But you know, in today's fast-paced world you sometimes wonder if there's anyone to reach out to.

Andrea: Having survived life on the streets, what programs and services do you think should be available for kids who are living in the street?

Victor: Drop-in centres, places where they know they can go without having any hassle, where they can look around and see non-threatening faces. Before you get an education, for a lot of kids, they've got to get their lives straightened out. It's pretty hard to sit there and concentrate on whatever it is that the teacher's writing on the blackboard when all you can think about is the crap that happened for the last two, three, four, five days at home. The thing is to have some kind of program that can first get the kid to deal with whatever problems he has at home or whatever it is that's bugging him.

Andrea: How did you turn things around for yourself?

Victor: Well, turning things around was a long, long, long process. At one point, I had to make a really hard decision to leave my buddies. They were the ones whose expectations I lived up to. And their expectations of me were as a fighter, a troublemaker. I realized when I was in detention in a solitary confinement cell that these weren't my friends. I was just living their impression of me. And I knew inside that my impression of me was totally different, that I wasn't a tough guy, that I didn't like the lifestyle I was in. I just got caught up in it.

And I didn't go back to my friends. I got a job and started hanging around with different people, but I wouldn't go out at night to the places I used to hang out in. I never touched those places again.

Once I was in newspapers, it was really odd because I found I couldn't go back to those places at all because I had basically, in the eyes of many of my former friends, crossed a line to the other side.

Andrea: Early in your autobiography, there is an account of your brother Freddie telling you to quit crying and you force yourself not to cry as you return to the boys home on a Sunday when your parents haven't come to visit. What's happened to all the tears that you haven't cried?

Victor: Just bottled them up. And I just made the decision, "Like hell, anyone's going to make me cry again." And I stopped it, whether it was my father or if someone punched me out, I just stood there and stared right in his face defiantly.

Andrea: Do they turn into anything, like rage?

Victor: Oh yeah, the rage was severe.

Andrea: What about your work? How does this fuel your work?

Victor: A lot of my work is not fueled by this pent-up rage. I think what's happened with my work over the years as a journalist is that I think about all of the injustices that were levelled on me and the boys that were in the home and their sisters who were in another home. And why did it happen and why was it allowed to be happening by a system that was out there and designed to care for kids who were less fortunate?

I use my anger and try not to forget that, try not to have my senses dulled because I happen to have a very comfortable life now. I find myself every so often feeling that my senses are dulled and I go back to the streets and do another story. Sure, I could write about politics or international events but suddenly you see me going back to the streets because you can't forget where you came from. And that starts my anger up again at the injustices of what's going on.

Andrea: What role does writing play in your life?

Victor: It puts me in touch with what's happening out in the world, particularly the situations that I was in. I don't sit there and look at it as a cathartic experience but I look at it as I'm doing something. I'm making a social statement and I think the social statement is the really important thing. I feel that although I cover a lot of stories now at *The 5th Estate,* I want to do stories primarily that make a social statement, that make an impact, that will create a few dents here and there for the better in the child welfare system, in the environment, in the political system, in education. Whatever I do a story in, if it makes a little dent and I feel that in writing you can do it, you can really, really do it.

Activities INTERVIEW WITH VICTOR MALAREK

■ Content and Style

1. Read the interview with a partner and list points that Malarek makes under the following two headings:
   - why teenagers ran away from home in the past
   - why they run away today

   Identify the main differences between the two lists. Compare your lists with another partnership. Then, as a group of four, brainstorm reasons for running away that do not appear in the interview.

2. Using information from the interview, list dangers and problems facing teens on the street. Add other dangers to the list that you feel might also exist. Compare your list with a partner's.

3. As a class, discuss Malarek's ideas about programs and services that could help young people in distress.
   a) Learn whether or not these programs are available in your community. You might find this information in your library, guidance department, or community health centre.
   b) List additional services you think should be available for street youth. Write a letter to the mayor of your community, explaining why your community needs the services.

■ Social Context

4. In many schools, there are senior students who live on their own. Arrange and conduct an interview with one or more of these young people. Share the information you obtain with classmates. Be sure to respect any wishes of people you interview to remain anonymous.

5. Read a fiction or non-fiction selection that describes the experiences of someone who has lived on the street. Write a summary of the selection in one or two paragraphs. (If the selection is long, you might focus on one section of it.) Present your summary to the class, stating whether or not you think the selection is worth reading.

6. Arrange for a guest speaker who has experience working with street youth to visit your class. Prepare questions in advance that you would like answered. Members of the class should introduce and thank the speaker.

■ Personal and Imaginative Response

7. Role play a conversation between a teenager who is thinking of living on the streets and a friend or adult with whom he or she is discussing the decision. Make it clear why the teenager wants to leave home, and have the friend or adult suggest some other possible actions.

8. Make a booklet for teenagers in distress that offers information, advice, and support. The booklet might be aimed at teens who are thinking of leaving home or teens who are already on the street. Invite a social worker or community services youth worker to provide feedback on the information in your booklet.

On the Sidewalk, Bleeding

BY EVAN HUNTER

The boy lay bleeding in the rain. He was sixteen years old, and he wore a bright purple silk jacket, and the lettering across the back of the jacket read THE ROYALS. The boy's name was Andy, and the name was delicately scripted in black thread on the front of the jacket, just over the heart. *Andy.*

He had been stabbed ten minutes ago. The knife had entered just below his rib cage and had been drawn across his body violently, tearing a wide gap in his flesh. He lay on the sidewalk with the March rain drilling his jacket and drilling his body and washing away the blood that poured from his open wound. He had known excruciating pain when the knife had torn across his body, and then suddenly comparative relief when the blade pulled away. He had heard the voice saying, "That's for you, Royal!" and then the sound of footsteps hurrying into the rain, and then he had fallen to the sidewalk, clutching his stomach, trying to stop the flow of blood.

He tried to yell for help, but he had no voice. He did not know why his voice had deserted him, or why the rain had become so suddenly fierce, or why there was an open hole in his body from which his life ran redly, steadily. It was 11:30 PM, but he did not know the time.

There was another thing he did not know.

He did not know he was dying. He lay on the sidewalk, bleeding, and he thought only: *That was a fierce rumble. They got me good that time,* but he did not know he was dying. He would have been frightened had he known. In his ignorance, he lay bleeding

109

and wishing he could cry out for help, but there was no voice in his throat. There was only the bubbling of blood from between his lips whenever he opened his mouth to speak. He lay silent in his pain, waiting, waiting for someone to find him.

He could hear the sound of automobile tires hushed on the muzzle of rainswept streets, far away at the other end of the long alley. He lay with his face pressed to the sidewalk, and he could see the splash of neon far away at the other end of the alley, tinting the pavement red and green, slickly brilliant in the rain.

He wondered if Laura would be angry.

He had left the jump to get a package of cigarettes. He had told her he would be back in a few minutes, and then he had gone downstairs and found the candy store closed. He knew that Alfredo's on the next block would be open until at least two, and he had started through the alley, and that was when he'd been ambushed. He could hear the faint sound of music now, coming from a long, long way off, and he wondered if Laura was dancing, wondered if she had missed him yet. Maybe she thought he wasn't coming back. Maybe she thought he'd cut out for good. Maybe she'd already left the jump and gone home. He thought of her face, the brown eyes and the jet-black hair, and thinking of her he forgot his pain a little, forgot that blood was rushing from his body. Someday he would marry Laura. Someday he would marry her, and they would have a lot of kids, and then they would get out of the neighborhood. They would move to a clean project in the Bronx, or maybe they would move to Staten Island. When they were married, when they had kids....

He heard footsteps at the other end of the alley, and he lifted his cheek from the sidewalk and looked into the darkness and tried to cry out, but again there was only a soft hissing bubble of blood on his mouth.

The man came down the alley. He had not seen Andy yet. He walked, and then stopped to lean against the brick of the building, and then walked again. He saw Andy then and came toward him, and he stood over him for a long time, the minutes ticking, ticking, watching him and not speaking.

Then he said, "What'sa matter, buddy?"

Andy could not speak, and he could barely move. He lifted his face slightly and looked up at the man, and in the rain-swept alley he smelled the sickening odor of alcohol and realized the man was drunk. He did not feel any particular panic. He did not know he was dying, and so he felt only mild disappointment that the man who had found him was drunk.

The man was smiling.

"Did you fall down, buddy?" he asked. "You mus' be as drunk as I am." He grinned, seemed to remember why he had entered the alley in the first place, and said, "Don' go way. I'll be ri' back."

The man lurched away. Andy heard his footsteps, and then the sound of the man colliding with a garbage can, and some mild swearing, and then the sound of the man urinating, lost in the steady wash of the rain. He waited for the man to come back.

It was 11:39.

When the man returned, he squatted alongside Andy. He studied him with drunken dignity.

"You gonna catch cold here," he said. "What'sa matter? You like layin' in the wet?"

Andy could not answer. The man tried to focus his eyes on Andy's face. The rain spattered around them.

"You like a drink?"

Andy shook his head.

"I gotta bottle. Here," the man said. He pulled a pint bottle from his inside jacket pocket. He uncapped it and extended it to Andy. Andy tried to move, but pain wrenched him back flat against the sidewalk.

"Take it," the man said. He kept watching Andy. "Take it." When Andy did not move, he said, "Nev' mind, I'll have one m'self." He tilted the bottle to his lips, and then wiped the back of his hand across his mouth. "You too young to be drinkin', anyway. Should be 'shamed of yourself, drunk an' layin' in a alley, all wet. Shame on you. I gotta good minda calla cop."

Andy nodded. Yes, he tried to say. Yes, call a cop. Please. Call one.

"Oh, you don't like that, huh?" the drunk said. "You don' wanna cop to fin' you all drunk an' wet in a alley, huh? Okay, buddy. This time you get off easy." He got to his feet. "This time you lucky," he said. He waved broadly at Andy, and then almost lost his footing. "S'long, buddy," he said.

Wait, Andy thought. *Wait, please, I'm bleeding.*

"S'long," the drunk said again. "I see you aroun'," and then he staggered off up the alley.

111

Andy lay and thought: *Laura, Laura. Are you dancing?*

The couple came into the alley suddenly. They ran into the alley together, running from the rain, the boy holding the girl's elbow, the girl spreading a newspaper over her head to protect her hair. Andy lay crumpled against the pavement, and he watched them run into the alley laughing, and then duck into the doorway not ten feet from him.

"Man, what rain!" the boy said. "You could drown out there."

"I have to get home," the girl said. "It's late, Freddie. I have to get home."

"We got time," Freddie said. "Your people won't raise a fuss if you're a little late. Not with this kind of weather."

"It's dark," the girl said, and she giggled.

"Yeah," the boy answered, his voice very low.

"Freddie…?"

"Um?"

"You're…you're standing very close to me."

"Um."

There was a long silence. Then the girl said, "Oh," only that single word, and Andy knew she'd been kissed, and he suddenly hungered for Laura's mouth. It was then that he wondered if he would ever kiss Laura again. It was then that he wondered if he was dying.

No, he thought, *I can't be dying, not from a little street rumble, not from just getting cut. Guys get cut all the time in rumbles. I can't be dying. No, that's stupid. That don't make any sense at all.*

"You shouldn't," the girl said.

"Why not?"

"I don't know."

"Do you like it?"

"Yes."

"So?"

"I don't know."

"I love you, Angela," the boy said.

"I love you, too, Freddie," the girl said, and Andy listened and thought: *I love you, Laura. Laura, I think maybe I'm dying. Laura, this is stupid but I think maybe I'm dying. Laura, I think I'm dying!*

He tried to speak. He tried to move. He tried to crawl toward the doorway where he could see the two figures in embrace. He tried to make a noise, a sound, and a grunt came from his lips, and then he tried again, and another grunt came, a low animal grunt of pain.

"What was that?" the girl said, suddenly alarmed, breaking away from the boy.

"I don't know," he answered.

"Go look, Freddie."

"No. Wait."

Andy moved his lips again. Again the sound came from him.

"Freddie!"

"What?"

"I'm scared."

"I'll go see," the boy said.

He stepped into the alley. He walked over to where Andy lay on the ground. He stood over him, watching him.

"You all right?" he asked.

"What is it?" Angela said from the doorway.

"Somebody's hurt," Freddie said.

"Let's get out of here," Angela said.

"No. Wait a minute." He knelt down beside Andy. "You cut?" he asked.

Andy nodded. The boy kept looking at him. He saw the lettering on the jacket then. THE ROYALS. He turned to Angela.

"He's a Royal," he said.

"Let's...what...what do you want to do, Freddie?"

"I don't know. I don't want to get mixed up in this. He's a Royal. We help him and the Guardians'll be down our necks. I don't want to get mixed up in this, Angela."

"Is he...is he hurt bad?"

"Yeah, it looks that way."

"What shall we do?"

"I don't know."

"We can't leave him here in the rain." Angela hesitated. "Can we?"

"If we get a cop, the Guardians'll find out who," Freddie said. "I don't know, Angela. I don't know."

Angela hesitated a long time before answering. Then she said, "I have to get home, Freddie. My people will begin to worry."

"Yeah," Freddie said. He looked at Andy again. "You all right?" he asked. Andy lifted his face from the sidewalk, and his eyes said: *Please, please help me,* and maybe Freddie read what his eyes were saying, and maybe he didn't.

Behind him, Angela said, "Freddie, let's get out of here! Please!" There was urgency in her voice, urgency bordering on the edge of panic. Freddie stood up. He looked at Andy again, and then

113

mumbled, "I'm sorry," and then he took Angela's arm and together they ran toward the neon splash at the other end of the alley.

Why, they're afraid of the Guardians, Andy thought in amazement. *But why should they be? I wasn't afraid of the Guardians. I never turkeyed out of a rumble with the Guardians. I got heart. But I'm bleeding.*

The rain was soothing somehow. It was a cold rain, but his body was hot all over, and the rain helped to cool him. He had always liked rain. He could remember sitting in Laura's house one time, the rain running down the windows, and just looking out over the street, watching the people running from the rain. That was when he'd first joined the Royals. He could remember how happy he was the Royals had taken him. The Royals and the Guardians, two of the biggest. He was a Royal. There had been meaning to the title.

Now, in the alley, with the cold rain washing his hot body, he wondered about the meaning. If he died, he was Andy. He was not a Royal. He was simply Andy, and he was dead. And he wondered suddenly if the Guardians who had ambushed him and knifed him had ever once realized he was Andy? Had they known that he was Andy, or had they simply known that he was a Royal wearing a purple silk jacket? Had they stabbed *him,* Andy, or had they only stabbed the jacket and the title, and what good was the title if you were dying?

I'm Andy, he screamed wordlessly. *I'm Andy, I'm Andy!*

An old lady stopped at the other end of the alley. The garbage cans were stacked there, beating noisily in the rain. The old lady carried an umbrella with broken ribs, carried it with all the dignity of a queen. She stepped into the mouth of the alley, a shopping bag over one arm. She lifted the lids of the garbage cans delicately, and she did not hear Andy grunt because she was a little deaf and because the rain was beating a steady relentless tattoo on the cans. She had been searching and foraging for the better part of the night. She collected her string and her newspapers, and an old hat with a feather on it from one of the garbage cans, and a broken footstool from another of the cans. And then she delicately replaced the lids and lifted her umbrella high and walked out of the alley mouth with queenly dignity. She had worked swiftly and soundlessly, and now she was gone.

The alley looked very long now. He could see people passing at the other end of it, and he wondered who the people were, and he wondered if he would ever get to know them, wondered who it was on the Guardians who had stabbed him, who had plunged the knife into his body.

"That's for you, Royal!" the voice had said, and then the footsteps, his arms being released by the others, the fall to the pavement. "That's for you, Royal!" Even in his pain, even as he collapsed, there had been some sort of pride in knowing he was a Royal. Now there was no pride at all. With the rain beginning to chill him, with the blood pouring steadily between his fingers, he knew only a sort of dizziness, and within the giddy dizziness, he could only think: *I want to be Andy.*

It was not very much to ask of the world.

He watched the world passing at the other end of the alley. The world didn't know he was Andy. The world didn't know he was alive. He wanted to say, "Hey, I'm alive! Hey, look at me! I'm alive! Don't you know I'm alive? Don't you know I exist?"

He felt weak and very tired. He felt alone and wet and feverish and chilled, and he knew he was going to die now, and the knowledge made him suddenly sad. He was not frightened. For some reason, he was not frightened. He was only filled with an overwhelming sadness that his life would be over at sixteen. He felt all at once as if he had never done anything, never seen anything, never been anywhere. There were so many things to do and he wondered why he'd never thought of them before, wondered why the rumbles and the jumps and the purple jacket had always seemed so important to him before, and now they seemed like such small things in a world he was missing, a world that was rushing past at the other end of the alley.

I don't want to die, he thought. *I haven't lived yet.*

It seemed very important to him that he take off the purple jacket. He was very close to dying, and when they found him, he did not want them to say, "Oh, it's a Royal." With great effort, he rolled over onto his back. He felt the pain tearing at his stomach when he moved, a pain he did not think was possible. But he wanted to take off the jacket. If he never did another thing, he wanted to take off the jacket. The jacket had only one meaning now, and that was a very simple meaning.

If he had not been wearing the jacket, he would not have been stabbed. The knife had not been plunged in hatred of Andy. The knife hated only the purple jacket. The jacket was a stupid

115

meaningless thing that was robbing him of his life. He wanted the jacket off his back. With an enormous loathing, he wanted the jacket off his back.

He lay struggling with the shiny wet material. His arms were heavy, and pain ripped fire across his body whenever he moved. But he squirmed and fought and twisted until one arm was free and then the other, and then he rolled away from the jacket and lay quite still, breathing heavily, listening to the sound of his breathing and the sound of the rain and thinking: *Rain is sweet, I'm Andy.*

She found him in the alleyway a minute past midnight. She left the dance to look for him, and when she found him she knelt beside him and said, "Andy, it's me, Laura."

He did not answer her. She backed away from him, tears springing into her eyes, and then she ran from the alley hysterically and did not stop running until she found the cop.

And now, standing with the cop, she looked down at him, and the cop rose and said, "He's dead," and all the crying was out of her now. She stood in the rain and said nothing, looking at the dead boy on the pavement, and looking at the purple jacket that rested a foot away from his body.

The cop picked up the jacket and turned it over in his hands.

"A Royal, huh?" he said.

The rain seemed to beat more steadily now, more fiercely.

She looked at the cop and, very quietly, she said, "His name is Andy."

The cop slung the jacket over his arm. He took out his black pad, and he flipped it open to a blank page.

"A Royal," he said.

Then he began writing.

■ Content and Style

1. With a partner, complete one of the following and present your conclusions to the class:
   - Identify each person who comes into the alley and could help Andy, and why each does not.
   - Determine why Andy wanted to join the Royals and why he wants to remove his jacket before he dies.
   - Discuss whether Andy and Laura had a real chance to have a happy life together.
   - Evaluate the behaviour of the police officer.

2. Write the message of the story in one or two sentences.

■ Social Context

3. In a group of four, brainstorm the meaning of the term *urban apathy*. Use a dictionary if necessary. Discuss whether or not you think this term applies to the story. Report your opinions to the class.

4. Write about whether or not being a member of a team, club, or gang is important to you. Explain your position.

■ Personal and Imaginative Response

5. Rewrite the incidents in this story as a radio or television script and tape a dramatized version of it.

6. Research the story of another pair of lovers, such as Pyramus and Thisbe or Romeo and Juliet, who were separated by death. Write a summary of the story and illustrate it using your own artwork or photographs clipped from magazines.

7. Write a news article about Andy's death that might have appeared in the paper the next day. Give it a suitable headline.

Interview With Peter Dalglish

BY ANDREA MOZAROWSKI

Peter Dalglish is the founder of Street Kids International (SKI). SKI works with street children throughout the developing world to help them build their self-respect and become independent. Born in London, Ontario, in 1957, Dalglish attended Upper Canada College where he was encouraged to *do* something, whether it meant joining the debating team or helping inner city kids. Later he studied at Stanford University in California and Dalhousie Law School in Nova Scotia. He was heading for a career in environmental law when the famine in Ethiopia in 1984 inspired him to take action. Since that time he has helped organize schooling for children in war-torn Sudan, created an adventure cartoon for children to teach them about AIDS, and now serves as executive director of Street Kids International. Believing in the power of individuals not institutions, Dalglish speaks for the rights and needs of street kids, war-affected kids, and kids in institutions. His philosophy could be summed up in the slogan on the bags the SKI couriers carry in Africa: "Not Tomorrow, Today."

Andrea: What made you finally say: "Enough is enough, I have to get involved"?

Peter: In October 1984, I was articling with a law firm in Halifax and I saw a picture of a kid in a refugee camp in Ethiopia. And I was determined that I was going to do something to help. So I organized an airlift of food and medical supplies to Ethiopia with my friend John Godfrey. And that led me to Ethiopia where I spent two weeks in refugee camps.

I guess that's when I realized that it wasn't going to be enough for me to practise law for eleven months of the year and take one month off to do something on the side. I was going to have to transform my life and make it a real lifetime commitment.

What fuels my work is rage. More than anything else, I feel rage. And it never goes away and it builds up. And I think that what I'm trying to do is channel that rage in a way that's constructive rather than letting it tear me apart.

Andrea: What impact do you think the mass media have on understanding these issues?

Peter: A huge impact, both good and bad. Good very much in terms of making people aware of some of the issues, maybe bringing people together, reducing distances. Only the mass media could mobilize people to respond the way they did for Band Aid, for example, in 1984, or Somalia in 1992, 1993 or Bosnia.

The mass media do put the spotlight on an issue, but they also tend to create in people a really short attention span. We can't focus on something for more than two or three weeks.

Andrea: How do the environments street kids find themselves in differ from country to country?

Peter: They do differ. Frankly, they're becoming a lot more similar, day by day, as urbanization reshapes the developing world. Things they have in common are lack of access to basic services, primarily health and education. Shelter is obviously a problem for the kids. Pollution is a growing problem. Barbarism, violence, physical and sexual abuse, these are all parts of their environment.

There are differences as well. Street youth in the north have a different existence than a lot of street youth in the south—not to say that it's any better in the north. But street youth in the north tend to be older. They also tend to be on the street for different reasons. In the south, traditionally kids are on the street because of poverty or because of war or catastrophe or something like that. In the north they tend to be on the streets because of a combination of abuse, often by someone who cares for them, quote, unquote.

So the kids take off like rockets. This is something that crosses all colours, income levels, and you find it everywhere.

Another thing they have in common is that family for these kids doesn't really exist. Maybe there's a mother somewhere or a grandparent. But for all intents and purposes, the family doesn't exist. There's a story about a famous street educator who was working with a bunch of kids. And this kid turned and started to run away. And the educator said, "Where are you running away to?" And the kid's response was, "To my mother, the street." It's a great idea—my mother, the street. It's a wonderful image.

Andrea: It's a painful image.

Peter: For a lot of the children, their mother or their father is the street. Another common characteristic is a lack of real positive role models, particularly male role models.

Andrea: When you make the children that you work with literate, how do their lives and futures change?

Peter: First of all, we don't make them literate, they make themselves literate. We help them become literate. And they become literate for good reason because they can earn more money. So, the first change is that they can earn a living. They become more independent, they have more self-esteem, they become much more in control of their environment. They become open to new opportunities. They take on responsibility to help teach other kids.

Andrea: Where do they go from there?

Peter: The best thing they can hope for probably is a job with the informal sector: a carpenter or a welder or an electrician. There will be all kinds of barriers to keep these kids from attending publicly funded schools. School uniform and school fee requirements effectively freeze poor children out of school. Another way is by requiring documentation of any kind like birth certificates—street children don't have birth certificates and they can never get them.

Andrea: The rights of children—how far have we come and what still needs to be done?

Peter: Not very far. We have the Convention of the Rights of the Child, which is a piece of paper. What the problem is, is that children have no rights essentially because they have no power, they have no vote. The Convention of the Rights of the Child has no enforcement provisions, no sanctions for nations that don't comply, no sanctions for those nations which sign, ratify, and then ignore. So it's only another piece of paper.

My own feeling that children have inherent rights has nothing to do with the Convention. They have inherent rights to be protected, to be loved, to an education, to receive basic shelter and health care. And I think if you don't provide those kids with those rights, you're violating the trust that the Creator placed with you as adults to care for children, not just your children but the world's children.

I think it's one of the great failures of our century that we're unable to care for our own children. When this century is judged, it won't be judged very well. Subsequent generations will wonder how we could have lived side by side with such poverty and not done anything about it.

Andrea: Do you ever feel like quitting or taking a break?

Peter: Taking a break? All the time. And I take lots of breaks. I took four weeks off this summer. Quitting? No. This is my life. I'll never quit. The world doesn't need another corporate lawyer. I think these kids, these dirty, foul-mouthed street kids deserve a lawyer of their own. And they're stuck with me.

You don't have to be a super human person to do this job. You can be a normal human being. In fact, I think what I'm doing is completely normal. I think to show some compassion for people in need is completely normal. It's what's expected. It's the least that you can do.

Activities   INTERVIEW WITH PETER DALGLISH

■ Content and Style

1. Identify three things Peter Dalglish says in the interview that suggest he really cares about young people in distress. Present and explain your choices to the class.

2. With a partner, describe what Dalglish means by the terms *north* and *south*. Write a paragraph describing what he considers to be the main differences between street youth in the north and the south.

3. Identify five things Dalglish suggests children need in order to become independent people with more self-esteem and control over their environment. Arrange your list to show which items are most important in your view. Share your list with the class, explaining the order of the items.

■ Social Context

4. Find examples of magazine advertisements and television programs that tell people about the problems of young people like the ones Dalglish describes. Choose one example and explain why you think the information it provides is or is not effective.

5. a) In a group, research and report on a large-scale fund-raising pro-
       ject, such as the 1984 Band Aid benefit to raise money for starv-
       ing people in Ethiopia. Your report should explain what caused
       the problem that needs funding, including social or political
       causes. If possible, include any recordings that were made to
       raise money.

    b) In a group, develop an idea for a fund-raising project to support a
       social problem you are concerned about. Decide on a marketing
       strategy. Describe the event and any performers or actors you
       would want to participate. You might suggest a theme song for
       the project.

■ Personal and Imaginative Response

6. Read the poem "Misery" on page 195. Write your own poem
    describing how you respond to television images of suffering
    children.

7. Write a description of what you might do to help the youth of your
    own community or in other parts of the world.

Those Who Don't

BY SANDRA CISNEROS

Those who don't know any better come into our neighborhood scared. They think we're dangerous. They think we will attack them with shiny knives. They are stupid people who are lost and got here by mistake.

But we aren't afraid. We know the guy with the crooked eye is Davey the Baby's brother, and the tall one next to him in the straw brim, that's Rosa's Eddie V. and the big one that looks like a dumb grown man, he's Fat Boy, though he's not fat anymore nor a boy.

All brown all around, we are safe. But watch us drive into a neighborhood of another color and our knees go shakity-shake and our car windows get rolled up tight and our eyes look straight. Yeah. That is how it goes and goes.

A Tanned Version

BY HUMMARAH QUDDOOS

And there is a huge immeasurable distance between us,
Between me and them.
They close their minds,
Ask the same repetitive questions,
Arranged marriages, strictness, trousers,
Same order.
Wherever I go.
What will they ask next:
Do you sleep, do you eat, can we touch?
I'm only a different colour
A tanned version of you.
They think we're all stereotypes
Carbon copies of each other.
We don't think they're all Princess Diana.
They're always amazed
When I can talk, can answer, have a mind,
As if to say this one's clever,
What other tricks do you do?
I'm not so very different
Just a tanned version of you.
How come I have to fight so hard
When you just have to show your face?

■ Content and Style

1. Although very different in form, these two selections have a similar message for the reader. Write this message in your notebook. Compare it with those written by classmates.

2. a) Describe the attitude of each of the narrators. Use information from the selections to support your opinion.

   b) With a partner, refer to each selection and discuss your reaction to the narrator's attitude. Consider which piece you like better and which attitude is most similar to your own. Share your ideas in a class discussion.

■ Social Context

3. a) In a small group, with the help of a dictionary, define the words *stereotyping* and *intimidation.*

   b) Write an explanation of how these two words could be used to describe what happens when a person enters an unfamiliar neighbourhood or meets someone from a different background.

4. With a partner, talk to an adult in counselling, co-operative education, or the office in your school about prejudice shown during a job interview. Find out about job interview questions that may not be asked and about the rights of the person being interviewed.

■ Personal and Imaginative Response

5. With a partner, create a storyboard for a commercial or a poster that illustrates the message conveyed by these two authors

   OR

   in a small group, find a display space in your school and design a visual presentation that will transmit the messages of these two writers.

6. Using either of the two selections as a model, write about a social issue that you think is a problem.

On a Very Gray Day

BY JANESSE LEUNG

On a very gray day, Katherine and I went shopping in Halifax. We combed through vintage clothing stores, music stores, expensive boutiques and import stores. We tried on millions of hats and jaywalked every chance we got. I treated her to lunch; we picked out a new restaurant, one with a jukebox, James Dean pictures on the walls and spotty spoons. Then I bought some transparent mascara because the regular kind makes my lashes fall out and we got a box of chocolates to share for dessert.

We walked back to the mall where my father had dropped us off before his meeting, passing businesslike people with black umbrellas and laughing at couples who dress the same (elbow, elbow, psst—look, twins…).

We ended up at a slide door in a glass-walled section of the mall, looking out on the circular drive of the hotel next door where my father would come to pick us up. He was late, so we sat on the steps inside and made up biographies for the people getting out of cars. One guy was fiddling around with a broken part of the curb and when he left he kept looking back at it as if it was going to come after him and attack the back of his neck. I thought it had something to do with a drug deal, but Katherine knows more about these things (she'd pointed a real one out to me earlier) and she didn't agree. We were annoyed by this time about having to wait so long, Katherine was supposed to be at home. I heard kids yelling above us from the main floor of the mall above the staircase where we were sitting, "…you ugly dogs…"

Katherine's voice broke through abruptly, oddly brittle. "C'mon. Let's go. There's your dad." I looked, but I didn't see our brown Volvo.

126

"Where? He's not there…" She was pulling me out the door but I heard the voices again, "…ugly dog in the pink coat…"

As I caught on, I felt my temper. It comes like a surge of adrenaline, short and impulsive and usually gone quickly. By then Katherine had propelled me out the door and almost around the corner, but I looked back and saw jeering eyes, curly brown hair and a stuck-out tongue through the glass. I felt ice water running through my veins and I raised my finger, sort of a reflex, and laughed without being amused. We walked slowly, very dignified, and the voices followed. "Stupid dog! Go clean your house, you smell like Chinese fish!"

I felt numb, my feet followed Katherine automatically. We turned another corner, out of sight and hearing, and she pushed me through a large swinging door marked "employees only" despite my protests. We stood on the other side leaning against a brick wall for a minute without speaking. I felt shock and embarrassment at my, ah, slightly less than mature and superior behaviour as well. But more than anything else, I had a surprising sense of sadness. Katherine and I looked at each other.

"Those kids were only seven or eight," I whispered. "I almost feel…sorry for them, for their not knowing any better."

"Yeah." She looked very self-possessed for a person who was hiding from a couple of little kids in an employees only area.

Suddenly I was afraid of leaving this shadowy brick hiding place. But Katherine stuck her head out cautiously, beckoned to me, and left. I followed, more reluctant to be left alone than to go back out. The kids following us had gone past our door which they thought we had also used. We went back to the glass-walled area. Katherine insisted that we stand under the staircase this time, the triangular space there was big and lighted but a bit dusty. I wanted to go back out, half hoping they would come back so I would have a second chance. From where we stood we were visible from outside but not from above. Katherine appeared dead calm, but she isn't a person who lets her emotions float on the surface. I had no idea what she was thinking.

After a while, my father arrived. I inflicted a little guilt on him for being so late, even though I knew that his meeting must have run late, as he explained it had. I sat next to Katherine in the back seat as we left Halifax, the trickle of Saturday traffic not a problem. She said nothing.

I wondered about the parents of those kids, the ones who had taught them or allowed them to say those things. Where I live, once in a while at school someone will say "chink" usually by accident, not addressing me. Heads snap around, all of a sudden we are the focal point of the room. He (why is it always a guy?) blushes and looks panic stricken. I say gently with a small smile, "Pardon me?" He mumbles something, I turn back to whatever I am doing. It has never happened more than once with the same person. There's almost no one at my school who isn't white, my friends tend to forget I'm not.

It's funny though, I think, "chink" isn't even a very accurate word for me. I'M only half Chinese. I'M tiny: only four feet, eleven and two-thirds inches (unfortunately), but I have natural-looking curly hair which is dark brown, not straight and black. I would look as different in Hong Kong or Beijing as I do here.

Katherine and I are both staring out the car windows in a vague, companionable silence. My father breaks it.

"Did you have a good day?" We smile at each other.

"Yes," I answer, "pretty good."

Activities ON A VERY GRAY DAY

■ Content and Style

1. With a partner, list the most important events that happened during the racist scene in the story. Compare your list with that of another partnership.

2. With a partner, discuss

   a) why the narrator says she would look as different in Hong Kong or Beijing as she does in Halifax, and

   b) why the narrator tells her father that the day was "pretty good."

   For each of (a) and (b), consider why the author included these details in the story. Summarize your discussion for the class.

■ Social Context

3. In a small group, discuss one of the topics below. Summarize your response and share it with the class.

   • In the story, the narrator says that she feels "shock and embarrassment" at her own behaviour. Explain why she feels this way and how else she and Katherine might have responded.

   • The story is set in the city of Halifax. Decide where an event like this is more likely to occur (i.e., large cities, smaller suburban communities, rural communities) and which people are more likely to be involved (i.e., children, teenagers, adults, senior citizens).

   • The narrator suggests that this kind of behaviour is more common to males than females. Decide whether you agree.

■ Personal and Imaginative Response

4. Describe a time you witnessed or experienced an event that caused a surge of anger or a sense of numbness similar to the one the narrator experienced.

5. Write a description of the day's events from the point of view of one of the yelling kids. Explain why you did what you did.

6. Imagine that the narrator told her father what happened instead of keeping it to herself. Write a new ending to the story based on what you think he would have said and/or done.

Capturing the Majesty of Nature

BY TYRONE CASHMAN

It takes only one summer for a child of the right age to bond with the natural world, to know in her bones that the world is alive and wild and kin to her. There is a kind of imprinting that either takes place or doesn't in a girl or boy before the age of 10 or 11.

As long as the wilderness survives, there is a place for this bonding to occur. As long as there are unspoiled natural places near enough for us to reach them and spend enough time in them, our children can have that inner awakening and sense of connection.

But it can never happen through media. Television's nature programs are wonderful. They must continue. They are probably the most important programming produced in our time. But we humans cannot form that essential bond through the tube.

The majesty, the power, the presence of a world uncreated by humans and uncorrupted by them cannot be reduced to the size of a TV screen, or glossy photographs in beautiful magazines, not even to the wrap-around screen of an Omni theater. Something essential is stripped from nature when it comes as a mediated image instead of a direct encounter.

When, for the first time, a nine-year-old barefoot boy and a wild crawfish encounter each other by surprise in a cold spring creek, there is nothing like it in the world. The boy's life is changed. And if he explores this watery world and the woods that surround it for the length of a long summer, he will have taken the whole ancient biosphere into his soul, never to be forgotten. The imprint is for a lifetime.

But if those imprintable years are allowed to pass for a boy or girl with only vicarious, mediated experience of nature, it is likely that as adults they will never be able to understand why a mountain forest is anything more than a pretty scene for a postcard or potential boardfeet or pulpwood for the commodities market.

■ Content and Style

1. a) List any words or phrases from the article that you do not under-
        stand. Add any words that you recognize but think the author
        used in an unusual way.
    b) As a class, talk about the meanings for the words you listed. Use a
        dictionary to help you.

2. a) In your own words, write the main point or argument the author
        presents in the article.
    b) List points the author uses to support his argument.

3. In a short paragraph, write what the author says can stop a young
    person from making a connection with nature. In a second para-
    graph, agree or disagree with the author's argument. Provide evi-
    dence to support your beliefs.

■ Social Context

4. In the second paragraph of the article, the authors says, "As long as
    there are unspoiled natural places near enough for us to reach them
    and spend enough time in them, our children can have that inner
    awakening and sense of connection." Write a short essay about how
    important it is for young people to connect with nature.

5. Look through several different kinds of magazines to find three to
    five advertisements that use scenes from nature to sell a product or
    idea or to make a point. In a paragraph, explain to what extent these
    advertisements encourage people to make connections with nature.

■ Personal and Imaginative Response

6. a) Take a walk in your schoolyard, local park, or ravine to note the
        sounds, sights, and smells of nature. Be aware of things you have
        never noticed before as well as things you notice regularly.
    b) Record your observations.
    c) Recreate the experience in a poem, a photo or sound collage, or a
        story.

As I Walk Along the Hillside *ancestors*

BY MISTY STANDS IN TIMBER

As I walk along the hillside,
I think about who my ancestors were
and how they lived.

I see tepees, and smoke
rising from them; the dry-meat poles
are filled,

buffalo hides being tanned,
children laughing, playing,
old men telling stories,
and young men become
warriors.
I hear the sound of drums beating

and people singing, dancing, eating.
I see horses grazing
on green grass in the meadow,
and as I walk along the hillside
I feel all these things inside me,
helping me to be who I am.

Tough Roots

BY JEAN MCCALLION

Dead as a stone? No.
These roots live.

Quickened by pulsing sun,
a rough tree vibrates outer warmth,

relays inner strength,
feels the tug of stubborn roots.

Unflinching under the lash of storms,
a tree remembers it held fast
when ice catapulted from far north
in lightning hails of thunder.

Isolated in back acres, concrete cities,
stubborn roots stone-contained

resist, no matter what machines
stutter angrily overhead
with great teeth.

Stopping by Woods on a Snowy Evening

BY ROBERT FROST   *snow*

Whose woods these are I think I know.
His house is in the village, though;
He will not see me stopping here
To watch his woods fill up with snow.

My little horse must think it queer
To stop without a farmhouse near
Between the woods and frozen lake
The darkest evening of the year.

He gives his harness bells a shake
To ask if there is some mistake.
The only other sound's the sweep
Of easy wind and downy flake.

The woods are lovely, dark, and deep,
But I have promises to keep,
And miles to go before I sleep,
And miles to go before I sleep.

Fear of the Landscape

BY IAN YOUNG

nature

On a hot morning
walking through rough thicket,
bushes and rocks
close to the bluffs
I was uneasy and clung to things.
The sound of a cricket
or the calls of birds were shrill
lesions in the quiet air
around me, sweltering and still.
The leaves hung from the trees
dangling on thin stems.

I am walking quickly and the land
stops. The ground
drops to a beach of stones
where a silent boat leans at the shore
into a sandy mound,
its stiff poled oars
outstretched.
The lake gulls circling it
cry out in the heat.
The sound of dry breath clings to me.
I hear the sun's core burn.
Have I been too long in cities
that I have such fear
of the landscape?

135

Jigsaw Discussion of Poems and Written Response to Poem of Choice

■ Expert Groups

1. Divide into four expert groups. Have each group choose one of the four poems to study. Each member of the group should keep notes on what is said about the poem.

2. Have each member of the group provide a response to the poem. Other members should not comment on these responses until everyone has spoken.

3. Discuss the poem and respond to comments made in the first round. Return to the poem to decide any differences of opinion that you may have. Consider the following:
   • the meaning of any difficult words and unclear statements
   • how nature is depicted
   • the relationship between the narrator and nature
   • any suggested relationship between human beings and nature

4. When you feel that you are finished, reread the poem to see if everything has been dealt with.

■ Sharing Groups

Form groups of four that include one expert on each poem. Have each expert read his or her poem aloud to the group and explain the ideas in the poem from his or her notes.

■ Personal Written Response

After you have talked about all the poems, choose the one that interests you most. Write a one-page response to it. Refer to details in the poem. Write in a way that will encourage your readers to read the poem themselves and discuss your response to it.

Healing the Planet

BY HELEN CALDICOTT

The only cure is love. I have just walked around my garden. It is a sunny, fall day, and white fleecy clouds are scudding across a clear, blue sky. The air is fresh and clear with no taint of chemical smells, and the mountains in the distance are ringed by shining silver clouds. I have just picked a pan full of ripe cherry guavas to make jam, and the house is filling with the delicate aroma of simmering guavas. Figs are ripening on the trees and developing that gorgeous deep red glow at the apex of the fruit. Huge orange-coloured lemons hang from the citrus trees, and lettuces, beetroots, and cabbages are growing in the vegetable garden. The fruit and vegetables are organically grown, and it feels wonderful to eat food that is free of artificial chemicals and poisons.

It is clear to me that unless we connect directly with the earth, we will not have the faintest clue why we should save it. We need to have dirt under our fingernails and to experience that deep, aching sense of physical tiredness after a day's labour in the garden to really understand nature. To feel the pulse of life, we need to spend days hiking in forests surrounded by millions of invisible insects and thousands of birds and the wonder of evolution. Of course, I realize that I am very fortunate indeed to be able to experience the fullness of nature so directly—literally in my own backyard. For many people—especially those living in urban areas who are unable to travel out of them regularly—such an experience is difficult to come by. Still, I urge all to try in some way to make a direct connection with the natural world.

Only if we understand the beauty of nature will we love it, and only if we become alerted to learn about the planet's disease processes can we decide to live our lives with a proper sense of ecological responsibility. And finally, only if we love nature, learn about its ills, and live accordingly will we be inspired to participate in needed legislative activities to save the earth. So my prescription for action to save the planet is, Love, learn, live, and legislate.

We must, then, with dedication and commitment, study the harm we humans have imposed upon our beloved earth. But this is not enough. The etiology of the disease processes that beset the earth is a byproduct of the collective human psyche and of the dynamics of society, communities, governments, and corporations that result from the innate human condition.

We have become addicted to our way of life and to our way of thinking. We must drive our cars, use our clothes dryers, smoke our cigarettes, drink our alcohol, earn a profit, look good, behave in a socially acceptable fashion, and never speak out of turn or speak the truth, for fear of rejection.

The problem with addicted people, communities, corporations, or countries is that they tend to lie, cheat, or steal to get their "fix." Corporations are addicted to profit and governments to power, and as Henry Kissinger once said, "Power is the ultimate aphrodisiac."

The only way to break addictive behaviour is to love and cherish something more than your addiction. When a mother and a father look into the eyes of their newborn baby, do they need a glass of beer or a cigarette to make them feel better? When you smell a rose or a gardenia, do you think of work or do you forget for a brief, blissful moment everything but the perfection of the flower? When you see the dogwood flowers hovering like butterflies among the fresh green leaves of spring, do you forget your worries?

Now, try to imagine your life without healthy babies, perfect roses, and dogwoods in spring. It will seem meaningless. We take the perfection of nature for granted, but if we woke up one morning and found all the trees dying, the grass brown, and the temperature 120°F [49°C], and if we couldn't venture outside because the sun would cause severe skin burns, we would recognize what we once had but didn't treasure enough to save.

To use a medical analogy: we don't really treasure our good health until we lose it or experience a dreadful accident. When I am injured, I always try immediately after the trauma, psychologically to recapture the moment before, when I was intact and healthy. But it is too late.

It is not too late, though, for our planet. We have ten years of work to do, and we must start now. If we don't, it may be too late for the survival of most species, including possibly, our own.

■ Content and Style

1. Write down the four actions that the author suggests we follow to heal the planet.

2. Explain to a partner why the author uses the word *addiction* to describe the environmental problems humans are causing. Have your partner explain what action the author suggests to break the addiction.

3. As a class, name the environmental problems that the author hints at but does not state. For example, "…we couldn't venture outside because the sun would cause severe skin burns…" is a reference to the thinning of the ozone layer.

4. With a partner, look up the meaning of the word *analogy* in the glossary. Then write an explanation of the analogy used in the second-last paragraph of the selection.

5. With a partner, list a word or phrase used in each paragraph that helps develop the medical analogy in the selection.

■ Social Context

6. a) As a class, discuss and chart the ways that individuals, businesses, and governments are adding to the ill health of the planet.

   b) Using the information, explain which group is most responsible for our environmental problems and which group is apt to become more environmentally sensitive first.

7. As a class, brainstorm the top ten problems facing the planet. Give evidence to support the seriousness of each problem. As an environmental doctor, write a prescription for healing the planet.

■ Personal and Imaginative Response

8. Write a description of a time you had a "direct connection with the natural world." Share it with classmates.

9. Create a two-part poster that contrasts an unhealthy planet with a healthy one. Include a title and five pieces of advice for making the planet healthy.

Living With Nature

BY DAVID SUZUKI

In spite of the vast expanse of wilderness in this country, most Canadian children grow up in urban settings. In other words, they live in a world conceived, shaped and dominated by people. Even the farms located around cities and towns are carefully groomed and landscaped for human convenience. There's nothing wrong with that, of course, but in such an environment, it's very easy to lose any sense of connection with nature.

In city apartments and dwellings, the presence of cockroaches, fleas, ants, mosquitoes or houseflies is guaranteed to elicit the spraying of insecticides. Mice and rats are poisoned or trapped, while the gardener wages a never-ending struggle with ragweed, dandelions, slugs and root-rot. We have a modern arsenal of chemical weapons to fight off these invaders and we use them lavishly.

We worry when kids roll in the mud or wade through a puddle because they'll get "dirty." Children learn attitudes and values very quickly and the lesson in cities is very clear—nature is an enemy, it's dirty, dangerous or a nuisance. So youngsters learn to distance themselves from nature and to try to control it. I am astonished at the number of adults who loathe or are terrified by snakes, spiders, butterflies, worms, birds—the list seems endless.

If you reflect on the history of humankind, you realize that for 99 per cent of our species' existence on the planet, we were deeply embedded in and dependent on nature. When plants and animals were plentiful, we flourished. When famine and drought struck, our numbers fell accordingly. We remain every bit as dependent upon nature today— we need plants to fix photons of energy into sugar molecules and to cleanse the air and replenish the oxygen. It is folly to forget our dependence on an intact ecosystem. But we do whenever we teach our offspring to fear or detest the natural world. The urban message kids get runs completely counter to what they are born with, a natural interest in other life forms. Just watch a child in a first encounter with a flower or an ant—there is instant interest and fascination. We condition them out of it.

The result is that when my 7-year-old daughter brings home new friends, they invariably recoil in fear or disgust when she tries to show them her favorite pets—three beautiful salamanders that her grandfather got for her in Vancouver. And when my 3-year-old comes wandering in with her treasures—millipedes, spiders, slugs and sowbugs that she catches under rocks lining the front lawn—children and adults alike usually respond by saying "yuk."

I can't overemphasize the tragedy of that attitude. For, inherent in this view is the assumption that human beings are special and different and that we lie outside nature. Yet it is this belief that is creating many of our environmental problems today.

Does it matter whether we sense our place in nature so long as we have cities and technology? Yes, for many reasons, not the least of which is that virtually all scientists were fascinated with nature as children and retained

that curiosity throughout their lives. But a far more important reason is that if we retain a spiritual sense of connection with all other life forms, it can't help but profoundly affect the way we act. Whenever my daughter sees a picture of an animal dead or dying, she asks me fearfully, "Daddy, are there any more?" At 7 years, she already knows about extinction and it frightens her.

The yodel of a loon at sunset, the vast flocks of migrating waterfowl in the fall, the indomitable salmon returning thousands of kilometres—these images of nature have inspired us to create music, poetry and art. And when we struggle to retain a handful of California condors or whooping cranes, it's clearly not from a fear of ecological collapse, it's because there is something obscene and frightening about the disappearance of another species at our hands.

If children grow up understanding that we are animals, they will look at other species with a sense of fellowship and community. If they understand their ecological place—the biosphere—then when children see the great virgin forests of the Queen Charlotte Islands being clearcut, they will feel physical pain, because they will understand that those trees are an extension of themselves.

When children who know their place in the ecosystem see factories

spewing poison into the air, water and soil they will feel ill because someone has violated their home. This is not mystical mumbo-jumbo. We have poisoned the life support systems that sustain all organisms because we have lost a sense of ecological place. Those of us who are parents have to realize the unspoken, negative lessons we are conveying to our children. Otherwise, they will continue to desecrate this planet as we have.

It's not easy to avoid giving these hidden lessons. I have struggled to cover my dismay and queasiness when Severn and Sarika come running in with a large wolf spider or when we've emerged from a ditch covered with leeches or when they have been stung accidentally by yellowjackets feeding on our leftovers. But that's nature. I believe efforts to teach children to love and respect other life forms are priceless.

■ Content and Style

1. In a group, create a glossary of the difficult words in the article. Share your glossary with other groups.

2. List five examples the author provides to show how the average city dweller dislikes nature. Make a second list of five ways human beings are dependent on nature. Compare your lists with those of another student.

3. As a class, select one sentence in this essay that summarizes its main idea or thesis.

■ Social Context

4. With a partner, identify something in nature that you dislike. Use the example you select as the focus of two role-playing activities that help explain the way humans respond to nature. In the first role play, perform a negative response. In the second role play, perform a positive response. Present your dramatizations to the class.

5. Create a list of five things parents could do with their children to help them develop a love and respect for nature.

6. Find another article or book by Suzuki and write a summary of one of the problems he presents.

■ Personal and Imaginative Response

7. Write a paragraph that describes your best experience with nature. Write a second paragraph that describes your worst experience. Then write one more paragraph to describe what you learned about nature through these experiences.

8. Find a book in a library that contains a good story, essay, or photo essay about humans interacting with nature. You might begin by looking at magazines such as *Outdoor Life, Backpacker,* and *Field and Stream.* Present your selection to the class and explain why you like it. You might also read a favourite section from it to your audience.

"Regular Guy" Becomes a Champion

BY FRANK JONES

Today, I'd like you to meet David Grassby, a 16-year-old Thornhill, Ontario, boy who never won any top academic prizes and who once played baseball for a team that was famous for being dead last. Even his dad Gerry describes David as "an ordinary boy."

He was ordinary, that is, until his teacher at St. Anthony Separate School, which he was attending four years ago when he was 12, handed out an assignment to come up with a science fair project.

Since then, David has appeared on radio and television numerous times, his name opens the doors of mayors and oil company presidents, and he has even had a play written about him, *The Champion of the Oakbank Pond*.

Drive a little west of old Thornhill and you'll see the pond. A historic plaque reminds us that J.E.H. MacDonald, one of the Group of Seven, lived on its banks from 1913 to 1932. With willows dipping their fronds in the water and ducks paddling by with their families, it seems a scene devised for a painter.

Except for the monster homes which have been allowed to intrude, in one case, right to the edge of the water. And they are only the visible part of the problem.

David learned to skate on Oakbank Pond. When David heard the pond's very existence was threatened, it was the cue for his science project.

He studied first how ponds maintain themselves, then dived into hefty reports that had already been prepared for the town of Vaughan—the kind of reports that flood across politicians' desks every week on their way to oblivion.

David boiled it down to four problems:
• Salt from nearby roads in winter was killing the zooplankton, the minute creatures which help to keep the water clear.

144

- Lawn fertilizers from nearby gardens were leaching into the ground water and causing an unsightly algae buildup.
- Because people were feeding the ducks, more and more ducks were arriving, their waste contaminating the water.
- The foundations for the big new houses, plus storm sewers, were cutting off the ground water that kept the pond from becoming stagnant.

David talked to environmentalist Pearl Shore, who was also concerned about the pond's future, and came up with answers to each of the problems:

- Sand should be used instead of salt on roads near the pond.
- People should switch to slow-release fertilizers on their lawns.
- Signs should be put up urging people not to feed the ducks.
- The ground water question was the hardest. David's suggestion: Vaughan council should force developers to put in storm sewers in ways which would not choke off the pond.

At the town's annual winter festival at the pond, David handed out questionnaires detailing the problems and asking people what they were prepared to do. Nearly everyone agreed to tell their friends about the pond, to write to the mayor, and to personally stop feeding the ducks.

David himself wrote to Mayor Lorna Jackson. His name was soon to become familiar to her. Soon he was calling her up, asking when the signs about the ducks were going up. Today you'll see them there, a tribute to David's persistence.

The town also agreed to spend $700 000 over four years to save the pond. So far, wells have been drilled along the shoreline.

Why did the politicians jump? They'd probably argue they were going to save the pond anyway.

The fact is that Lesley Simpson, then a reporter for *The Star,* spotted David handing out his questionnaires at the winter carnival and wrote about him. Soon David was making regular appearances on CBC radio programs. One morning he got up at 5 AM with his dad and went to the CITY-TV studio to tell his story on the morning show.

The biggest thrill came when one of his heroes, environmentalist David Suzuki, came to Thornhill to film a sequence with David at Oakbank Pond for a TV special. A signed photograph of himself with Suzuki is one of his proudest possessions.

No one was more amazed at all this than his parents, Donna and Gerry. David was never the guy who spoke up in class or stood out in any special way.

"He was just like his father—a real, regular guy," says Gerry. "We were amazed that he had this spark, that he was not going to be put off by people."

145

Playwright Jim Betts heard David on the radio one day and thought he'd be an ideal subject for a musical for Theatre on the Move. Based at Black Creek Pioneer Village, the troupe tours schools. A lengthy collaboration with David followed, culminating in a highly successful tour of 110 schools this spring.

Donna shed a tear the first time she saw it.

"It suddenly occurred to me what he had actually done," she says. "How many people have a song or a play written about them!"

You'd expect a boy getting that kind of exposure to become, well, just a bit full of himself. Not David.

"I always tried to stick to the original purpose: getting the community to save the pond," he says.

Another break came his way when his principal at St. Robert Catholic high school, Gerry Brand, permitted him to take a week off to tour with the play. He was asked to sign autographs and one eighth grader told him, "We're really proud of you."

But David was getting the most excitement backstage. Theatre lighting is his hobby, and he took me down to the basement to show me a lighting system he invented and wired himself. So when they told him he could help the stage manager, it almost beat the pleasure of seeing actor Drew Carnwath playing him onstage. Almost.

The musical launches with a song called "Anyone can make a difference." Everything that's happened, says Gerry, a business consultant, "has been a gift to David in terms of his self-confidence and his recognition that he is a person who counts, who has something to give to his community and his friends. You can be an ordinary guy and still make a contribution."

Activities   "REGULAR GUY" BECOMES A CHAMPION

■ Content and Style

1. Write a description of the events that changed David Grassby from a "regular guy" to the subject of a play.

2. Write a paragraph explaining what you admire most about David. In a group of four, read your paragraphs aloud to see whether you made similar or different choices.

3. A science fair project is meant to be a learning experience. As a class, discuss the lessons David learned from his project.

■ Social Context

4. In a group of four, list ways the media and politicians helped David. Make a second list explaining how they used David for their own purposes. Decide whether the politicians and the media in this story are the good guys or the bad guys. Compare your decision with that of other groups.

5. a) As a class, identify an environmental problem in your community and brainstorm what you could do to draw attention to it.

   b) Establish a class committee to follow through on at least one of your ideas.

■ Personal and Imaginative Response

6. Write about a time when you or your friends did something to help the community, such as joining a volunteer program.

7. Ask your librarian or art teacher to help you find books of paintings by J.E.H. MacDonald, A. Y. Jackson, or another member of the Group of Seven. Show your favourite picture to the class and explain why you chose it.

The Iguana

BY ISAK DINESEN

In the Reserve I have sometimes come upon the iguanas, the big lizards, as they were sunning themselves upon a flat stone in a riverbed. They are not pretty in shape, but nothing can be imagined more beautiful than their colouring. They shine like a heap of precious stones or like a pane cut out of an old church window. When, as you approach, they swish away, there is a flash of azure, green and purple over the stones; the colour seems to be standing behind them in the air, like a comet's luminous tail.

Once I shot an iguana. I thought that I should be able to make some pretty things from his skin. A strange thing happened then, that I have never afterwards forgotten. As I went up to him, where he was lying dead upon his stone, and actually while I was walking the few steps, he faded and grew pale; all colour died out of him as in one long sigh, and by the time that I touched him he was grey and dull like a lump of concrete. It was the live impetuous blood pulsating within the animal which had radiated out all that glow and splendour. Now that the flame was put out, and the soul had flown, the iguana was as dead as a sandbag.

Often since I have, in some sort, shot an iguana, and I have remembered the one of the Reserve. Up at Meru I saw a young Native girl with a bracelet on, a leather strap two inches wide, and embroidered all over with very small turquoise-coloured beads which varied a little in colour and played in green, light blue and ultramarine. It was an extraordinarily live thing; it seemed to draw breath on her arm, so that I wanted it for myself, and made Farah buy it from her. No sooner had it come upon my own arm than it gave up the ghost. It was nothing now, a small, cheap, purchased article of finery. It had been the play of colours, the duet between

148

the turquoise and the quick, brownish black of the Native's skin that had created the life of the bracelet.

In the Zoological Museum of Pietermaritzburg, I have seen, in a stuffed deep-water fish in a showcase, the same combination of colouring, which there had survived death; it made me wonder what life can well be like, on the bottom of the sea, to send up something so live and airy. I stood in Meru and looked at my pale hand and at the dead bracelet. It was as if an injustice had been done to a noble thing, as if truth had been suppressed. So sad did it seem that I remembered the saying of the hero in a book that I had read as a child: "I have conquered them all, but I am standing amongst graves."

In a foreign country and with foreign species of life one should take measures to find out whether things will be keeping their value when dead. To the settlers of East Africa I give the advice: "For the sake of your own eyes and heart, shoot not the iguana."

Activities   THE IGUANA

■ Content and Style

1. List any words in the story that you do not understand. Share your list with a partner. Using the context of the words in the story and a dictionary, determine and record the meaning of these words.

2. List adjectives that you would use to describe the act of shooting the iguana. List adjectives to describe the act of buying the bracelet. With a partner, share your lists. Decide what the author learns after her experience of shooting the iguana and buying the bracelet.

3. a) In the fourth paragraph, the author says, "I have seen, in a stuffed deep-water fish in a showcase, the same combination of colouring, which there had survived death...." As a class, consider why the author might have included this detail.

   b) Discuss the significance of the quotation at the end of this paragraph.

■ Social Context

4. a) This story is taken from a volume of stories entitled *Out of Africa*. Do some research to find out who Isak Dinesen was and what her life was like.

   b) If you can find the collection in the library, read another story from *Out of Africa*. Share your responses to it with classmates.

5. As Dinesen, using "The Iguana" as your reference, write a speech updating your message for people today.

■ Personal and Imaginative Response

6. a) Choose ten words from the story that appeal to you. Use these words in a poem. The poem does not have to tell a story or be related to "The Iguana."

   b) Read your poem to the class.

   c) After hearing the poems of your classmates, discuss the ideas the poems have in common and how the poems are different.

7. a) Write a fable entitled "The Hunter and the Iguana," in which an iguana speaks with a hunter who wants to kill it.

   b) In a group, dramatize one iguana fable for the class

   OR

   use your fable as the basis of a picture book for children.

December 2001: The Green Morning

BY RAY BRADBURY

When the sun set, he crouched by the path and cooked a small supper and listened to the fire crack while he put the food in his mouth and chewed thoughtfully. It had been a day not unlike thirty others, with many neat holes dug in the dawn hours, seeds dropped in, and water brought from the bright canals. Now, with an iron weariness in his slight body, he lay and watched the sky colour from one darkness to another.

His name was Benjamin Driscoll, and he was thirty-one years old. And the thing that he wanted was Mars grown green and tall with trees and foliage, producing air, more air, growing larger with each season; trees to cool the towns in the boiling summer, trees to hold back the winter winds. There were so many things a tree could do: add colour, provide shade, drop fruit, or become a children's playground, a whole sky universe to climb and hang from; an architecture of food and pleasure, that was a tree. But most of all the trees would distil an icy air for the lungs, and a gentle rustling for the ear when you lay nights in your snowy bed and were gentled to sleep by the sound.

He lay listening to the dark earth gather itself, waiting for the sun, for the rains that hadn't come yet. His ear to the ground, he could hear the feet of the years ahead moving at a distance, and he imagined the seeds he had placed today sprouting up with green and taking hold on the sky, pushing out branch after branch, until Mars was an afternoon forest, Mars was a shining orchard.

In the early morning, with the small sun lifting faintly among the folded hills, he would be up and finished with a smoky breakfast in a few minutes and, trodding out the fire ashes, be on his way with knapsacks, testing, digging, placing seed or sprout, tamping lightly,

151

watering, going on, whistling, looking at the clear sky brightening toward a warm noon.

"You need the air," he told his night fire. The fire was a ruddy, lively companion that snapped back at you, that slept close by with drowsy pink eyes warm through the chilly night. "We all need the air. It's a thin air here on Mars. You get tired so soon. It's like living in the Andes, in South America, high. You inhale and don't get anything. It doesn't satisfy."

He felt his rib case. In thirty days, how it had grown. To take in more air, they would all have to build their lungs. Or plant more trees.

"That's what I'm here for," he said. The fire popped. "In school they told a story about Johnny Appleseed walking across America planting apple trees. Well, I'm doing more. I'm planting oaks, elms, and maples, every kind of tree, aspens and deodars and chestnuts. Instead of making just fruit for the stomach, I'm making air for the lungs. When those trees grow up some year, *think* of the oxygen they'll make!"

He remembered his arrival on Mars. Like a thousand others, he had gazed out upon a still morning and thought, How do I fit here? What will I do? Is there a job for me?

Then he had fainted.

Someone pushed a vial of ammonia to his nose and, coughing, he came around.

"You'll be all right," said the doctor.

"What happened?"

"The air's pretty thin. Some can't take it. I think you'll have to go back to Earth."

"No!" He sat up and almost immediately felt his eyes darken and Mars revolve twice around under him. His nostrils dilated and he forced his lungs to drink in deep nothingnesses. "I'll be all right. I've got to stay here!"

They let him lie gasping in horrid fishlike motions. And he thought, Air, air, air. They're sending me back because of air. And he turned his head to look across the Martian fields and hills. He brought them to focus, and the first thing he noticed was that there were no trees, no trees at all, as far as you could look in any direction. The land was down upon itself, a land of black loam, but nothing on it, not even grass. Air, he thought, the thin stuff whistling in his nostrils. Air, air. And on top of hills, or in their shadows, or even by little creeks, not a tree and not a single green blade of grass. Of course! He felt the answer came not from his mind, but his lungs and his throat. And the thought was like a sudden gust of pure oxygen, raising him up. Trees and grass. He looked down at his hands and turned them over. He would plant trees and grass. That would be his job, to fight against the very thing that might prevent his staying here. He would have a private horticultural war with Mars. There lay the old soil, and the plants of it so ancient they had worn themselves out. But what if new forms were introduced? Earth trees, great mimosas and weeping willows and magnolias and magnificent eucalyptus. What then? There was no guessing what mineral wealth hid in the soil, untapped because the old ferns, flowers, bushes, and trees had tired themselves to death.

"Let me up!" he shouted. "I've got to see the Co-ordinator!"

He and the Co-ordinator had talked an entire morning about things that grew and were green. It would be months, if not years, before organized planting began. So far, frosted food was brought from Earth in flying icicles; a few community gardens were greening up in hydroponic plants.

"Meanwhile," said the Co-ordinator, "it's your job. We'll get what seed we can for you, a little equipment. Space on the rockets is mighty precious now. I'm afraid, since these first towns are mining communities, there won't be much sympathy for your tree planting—"

"But you'll let me do it?"

They let him do it. Provided with a single motorcycle, its bin full of rich seeds and sprouts, he had parked his vehicle in the valley wilderness and struck out on foot over the land.

That had been thirty days ago, and he had never glanced back. For looking back would have been sickening to the heart. The weather was excessively dry; it was doubtful if any seeds had sprouted yet. Perhaps his entire campaign, his four weeks of bending and scooping were lost. He kept his eyes only ahead of him, going on down this wide shallow valley under the sun, away from First Town, waiting for the rains to come.

Clouds were gathering over the dry mountains now as he drew his blanket over his shoulders. Mars was a place as unpredictable as time. He felt the baked hills simmering down into frosty night, and he thought of the rich, inky soil, a soil so black and shiny it almost crawled and stirred in your fist, a rank soil from which might sprout gigantic beanstalks from which, with bone-shaking concussion, might drop screaming giants.

The fire fluttered into sleepy ash. The air tremored to the distant roll of a cartwheel. Thunder. A sudden odor of water. Tonight, he thought, and put his hand out to feel for rain. Tonight.

He awoke to a tap on his brow.

Water ran down his nose into his lips. Another drop hit his eye, blurring it. Another splashed his chin.

The rain.

Raw, gentle, and easy, it mizzled out of the high air, a special elixir, tasting of spells and stars and air, carrying a peppery dust in it, and moving like a rare light sherry on his tongue.

Rain.

He sat up. He let the blanket fall and his blue denim shirt spot, while the rain took on more solid drops. The fire looked as though an invisible animal were dancing on it, crushing it, until it was angry smoke. The rain fell. The great black lid of sky cracked in six powdery blue chips, like a marvelous crackled glaze, and rushed down. He saw ten billion rain crystals, hesitating long enough to be photographed by the electrical display. Then darkness and water.

He was drenched to the skin, but he held his face up and let the water hit his eyelids, laughing. He clapped his hands together and stepped up and walked around his little camp, and it was one o'clock in the morning.

It rained steadily for two hours and then stopped. The stars came out, freshly washed and clearer than ever.

Changing into dry clothes from his cellophane pack, Mr. Benjamin Driscoll lay down and went happily to sleep.

The sun rose slowly among the hills. It broke out upon the land quietly and wakened Mr. Driscoll where he lay.

He waited a moment before arising. He had worked and waited a long hot month, and now, standing up, he turned at last and faced the direction from which he had come.

It was a green morning.

As far as he could see the trees were standing up against the sky. Not one tree, not two, not a dozen, but the thousands he had planted in seed and sprout. And not little trees, no, not saplings, not little tender shoots, but great trees, huge trees, trees as tall as ten men, green and green and huge and round and full, trees shimmering their metallic leaves, trees whispering, trees in a line over hills, lemon trees, lime trees, redwoods and mimosas and oaks and elms and aspens, cherry, maple, ash, apple, orange, eucalyptus, stung by a tumultuous rain, nourished by alien and magical soil and, even as he watched, throwing out new branches, popping open new buds.

"Impossible!" cried Mr. Benjamin Driscoll.

But the valley and the morning were green.

And the air!

All about, like a moving current, a mountain river, came the new air, the oxygen blowing from the green trees. You could see it shimmer high in crystal billows. Oxygen, fresh, pure, green, cold oxygen turning the valley into a river delta. In a moment the town doors would flip wide, people would run out through the new miracle of oxygen, sniffing, gusting in lungfuls of it, cheeks pinking with it, noses frozen with it, lungs revivified, hearts leaping, and worn bodies lifted into a dance.

Mr. Benjamin Driscoll took one long deep drink of green water and air and fainted.

Before he woke again five thousand new trees had climbed up into the yellow sun.

Activities   DECEMBER 2001: THE GREEN MORNING

■ Content and Style

1. List several key words that are repeated in this story. Compare your list with a partner's, and decide why the author used them repeatedly.

2. In a group, discuss facts about Mars that you knew previous to reading this story. List the facts the author includes in his story. List other information that you would like to learn.

3. Select a descriptive paragraph in the story to read to a partner. After you read it, explain why you chose it.

4. Working with a partner, role play the following:
   - the conversation between the Co-ordinator and Benjamin Driscoll that ends in Driscoll being given permission to plant trees
   - the conversation between the two when Driscoll returns from his planting trip

■ Social Context

5. Although the story takes place on a Mars of the future, there is a message in it for our society. In your notebook, write two or more sentences to explain the message.

6. Make the following two lists:
   - the benefits of space travel
   - the disadvantages of space travel

   In a group of four, discuss your lists and decide whether you, as a committee of the government, would provide the funds for future space travel.

■ Personal and Imaginative Response

7. On the basis of this story and any other information you might have, write a letter to the co-ordinator of the Canadian Space Agency. Explain why you would or would not like to live in a space colony on Mars.

8. Write a poem about what a tree can do, using the ideas suggested in the second paragraph of the story. Transfer your poem to a large sheet of paper and illustrate it.

9. Describe your favourite science fiction and/or fantasy story, film, or television show. Explain why it is your favourite. Share your description with a partner.

1. In a group of four, choose an issue from this unit that has two opposing sides. Form two teams of two and hold a debate on the issue. (See page 81 for the rules of debating.)

2. Some of the ideas presented in this unit include the following:
   - dealing with racism
   - understanding the culture of the mall
   - learning about the experiences of street youth

   In a group, brainstorm a list of ideas for getting along in an urban environment. Put together a guidebook of tips for living in this environment.

3. For two weeks, clip newspaper articles on environmental issues. Create a scrapbook and write an overview of the most serious issue that was covered in the two-week period.

4. Make a photographic exhibit or video documentary about one of the most beautiful environments in your community or the most environmentally threatened spot in your community.

5. Prepare a slide show on an environment that you find interesting. Photograph architecture, landscaping, colour, and other details that illustrate what this environment means to you.

6. In a group, design an environment that you think would be good for teenagers. You might focus on a place to go to instead of a mall, or design an entire community. Brainstorm ideas about what to include. The finished design should include a labelled drawing of the environment and an explanation of its features. Present your design to the class and invite responses to it.

7. a) Examine the selections in the unit about the natural environment that encourage people to connect with the earth. Decide which selection appeals to you the most. Write a summary of the message of this selection and why you found it persuasive. Share your response with a partner.

   b) Decide what you think is your own connection with the earth and how you might express this connection. You might consider writing a series of poems, creating a sound collage, writing an article for a local newspaper, or taking photographs and creating a display.

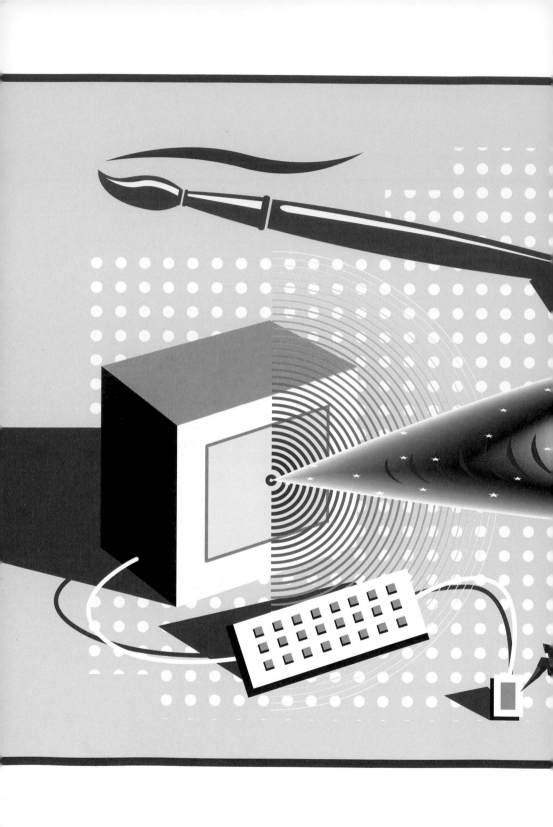

EXPRESSING

YOURSELF

IN A

HIGH-TECH

WORLD

A Warm Safe Bed

BY MONICA HUGHES

We got an assignment in Holistic English today: *My Roots and What They Mean to Me*. It's to be partly a research project and partly an exercise in the "literary convention of the essay." The results will make up fifty per cent of our final mark, so it's pretty important.

My roots: I guess I'm lucky. My father's family is from Trinidad and my mother's is from Japan. He's a famous Caribbean musician and composer. You've probably heard of Dirk Johnson. Mum's a mathematician, the kind who doesn't deal in numbers, but mostly Greek letters that describe how the universe began and where it's going.

Parents like mine make for fascinating conversation at the breakfast table and, like I say, I'm lucky. I love every kind of music, and maths is a snap. I'm also pretty good at English, which neither of them care about at all.

Physically, my parents' genes have made me a hundred and fifty centimetres tall, and I weigh an even fifty kilogrammes in a bikini, which really becomes me. I have small bones and my skin is the colour of nicely-done toast. My eyes are dark and my hair is black and wavy, but not unmanageable. Altogether, a neat package; I'm glad I'm me.

When I explained to Mum about my assignment, she gave me the access code to the file she calls, "Family Album." It's fascinating: Mum's family history, generation by generation back to Osaka, Japan. Pictures of her grandparents' wedding, with him in a stiff-collared black suit and her in a gorgeous kimono, her piled-up hair full of ornaments. Mum's mother and father were married in Clapham, and their clothes were ordinary, only a bit old-fashioned.

Dad's father ran away from Trinidad to Liverpool, so there's not a

160

lot of history and pictures of his side of the family in the file, just a couple of snaps of him as a young man and the wedding photographs which I recognised, of course, from the holograms on the living-room wall.

The next item was their marriage certificate: June 4, 1992, and my birth certificate, November 3, 1994. Me, Naoko, the only child.

"Didn't you want a boy as well?" I used to ask, when I was younger, thinking it might be fun to have a kid brother to boss around. But Mum and Dad always shook their heads and said they were lucky to get me.

My Roots and What They Mean to Me. I could write ten pages, I guess, but I knew I wouldn't get high marks for research that way. I decided that since I had access to "Family Album," I'd look for an interesting angle. I wasn't actually snooping. At least it didn't seem that way at the time. But when I came to Mum's personal medical history I just peeked. Honest, that's all.

Surprise! Wow! In 1991, before I was born, before Mum had even met Dad, she had had a hysterectomy. If it meant what I thought it meant then Mum couldn't have possibly had any babies. She couldn't have had *me*.

I'm adopted! That was my first thought, my head in a whirl. But my eyes, my high cheekbones, the dimple just like Mum's, all denied that possibility. If you'd overlaid a transparency of Mum and one of Dad, the resulting double image was ME.

I had just enough presence of mind to exit the program properly before resetting the privacy code and switching off. Then I went for a long walk, round and round the apartment blocks, my heart pounding like mad and my hands all sweaty, like before a history exam. I thought up some pretty wild scenarios as I walked, like Dad having an affair with Mum's twin sister, and Mum nobly adopting the baby—though, as far as I knew, Mum had no sisters at all, much less a twin. *Who am I?* I asked the dustbins and the skinny trees. *Where did I come from?*

Naturally the dustbins and trees had no answer and, in the end, totally confused, with my knees trembling partly from all that pavement pounding and partly from sheer nerves, I did what I should have done in the first place. I went into the kitchen where Mum was chopping vegetables and chicken for supper.

"Mum, where do I *really* come from?"

She laid the chopper down on the block and stared at me, her face so like mine. "Naoko, what do you mean? You know who your grandparents are and your great…"

"I don't mean that. I mean me, myself." And I explained about peeking into her medical file. At the expression on her face I felt about fifty centimetres high. She looked shocked, outraged, and maybe a little scared. What horrible secret *was* there about me?

"Sorry, Mum," I muttered. "I guess I shouldn't have."

"Slice the mushrooms," was all she said, her lips tight, putting a knife into my hand.

We worked together in a silence broken only by the whack of Mum's cleaver on the block. "You are our very own child," she said at last. "My ovum. Your father's sperm. You are truly ours. But you had a surrogate mother, that's all."

"I see," I said, not seeing at all. I sliced the mushrooms into thin, even slices with great concentration, as if my life depended on it. I just stared at those mushrooms, so I knew each pinky-brown gill by heart. When I'd finished and Mum had begun the stir-fry, I ran to my room and looked up "surrogate" in the dictionary.

Surrogate: a substitute, a deputy.

Surrogate mother: a woman in whose uterus the zygote (fertilized egg) of another couple is implanted and raised to maturity.

Surrogate Laws: see R. versus Hepplethwaite, 1991.

I put the book back on the shelf and thought about it. Me. "Implanted and raised to maturity." It was like a bad dream. I'll wake up and it'll just be a bizarre dream, I told myself. Or a joke. Mum's just having me on.

If it *were* true, there was still one major problem, so I brought it up at supper, kind of testing Mum. If it *were* a joke, she'd have to tell me then.

"How can an egg possibly get fertilized before it's put into the surrogate mother?"

Dad choked, gulped his guava juice and choked again.

"Really, Naoko!"

"Sorry, Mum, but I need to know. How does it?"

"You've heard of test-tube babies, haven't you?" Dad wiped his eyes on his napkin.

"Which is a misnomer," Mum put in severely. "As you well know, Dirk. Technically, Naoko, you were conceived in a Petri dish." She didn't say any more and I knew she was still hurt that I'd snooped in her private file.

"Thanks, Mum," I said weakly. So it was true. There was something particularly real and scientific and definite about a Petri dish. I thought about it, as I silently stacked the plates in the dishwasher. A *Petri* dish!

"Conceived in a *dish!*" I said to my reflection in the bathroom mirror as I brushed my teeth. "There's romance for you!"

It was the kind of situation that would make a great joke. I imagined heading my essay: *My Roots in a Dish.* Or possibly *The Dish and I.* But all the time my brain was being flip and funny, inside my stomach was trembly and full of butterflies.

I'd always known that my parents really loved each other, romantically as well as being good and favourite friends, and it had always given me a warm glow to think about *me*, toasty skin and wavy hair, music and maths, like the seal of approval on their love.

Now that was all gone. Zip. Finished. Sure, I still had two loving parents who'd raised me since I was born. But I couldn't relate to that Petri dish. No way! That was science. As sterile and impersonal as the laboratory where I supposed it happened. I jumped into bed and lay there, wondering what had happened to my secure world.

When Mum came in to kiss me good night I didn't link my hands behind her neck and pull her down on top of me in a bear hug the way I always did, even though I was almost fifteen and really too big for bear hugs. I lay on my back and looked up at her, and she looked down at me, a little sadly, the way I felt inside, as if she were my reflection.

"I suppose you had to bottle-feed me, too," I said, accusingly.

"I certainly did not!"

"Did I have a surrogate *nurse* too?" I hadn't meant for the words to sound that odious, but they did and Mum turned away to the window, pretending to fix the curtain. She is very stoical, the way Japanese people are still brought up to be, and she *never* shows her emotions unless she wants to.

After a while fixing the curtain she said, very softly, so I could hardly hear her, "*I* nursed you, Naoko. The doctor gave me hormones and I nursed you for six months."

"Oh," was the only thing I could think of to say. Afterwards I thought I could have said I was sorry and that it was all right, but just then I was angry and I wanted an excuse to stay angry.

Mum turned back from the window. She kissed my forehead and I think she paused, just for a second, in case I should pull her

163

down into a bear hug, but I wouldn't. She straightened up, said, "Good night, Naoko," and slipped out of the room like a quiet, drooping shadow.

I lay awake, my hands behind my head, staring at the ceiling, thinking about my mother. My surrogate mother, I mean. The one who had nourished me, with whom I had spent the first nine months of my life. I wondered what she was like. Would she be Oriental, like Mum? Or Caribbean, like Dad? I wondered if she'd have minded dreadfully having to give me up after nine months of pregnancy and labour and all that stuff? I had been a beautiful baby. I'm not just saying that. I know it's true because of everyone's reactions to my baby pictures in the living room. If I had been she, I'd *never* have given me up. I couldn't.

I lay, staring at the ceiling, as the clock numbers turned briskly over from 23:00 to 01:05 to 02:10. Now I felt rejected. By Mum and Dad who had caused me to be created in a Petri dish. And by the person I was beginning to think of as "my real mother."

What sort of woman would raise another couple's baby and then give it back, newborn and gorgeously, miraculously, alive? Perhaps she was a noble friend, sacrificing her life to bring happiness to Mum and Dad. I liked that idea and I wondered if Mum would tell me if I asked her.

What was she like? Perhaps she was an artist. Or maybe a famous writer. Did I get my love of language from her? After all, I argued to myself, you can't be an intimate part of a person for nine whole months and not be influenced by them. Maybe she read poetry to me before I was born. I *love* poetry most passionately and I write some, though I don't feel like showing it to anyone, not yet.

Did she ever think of me, my surrogate mother? Did she miss me? *Would she like to see me again?* With this momentous question, I sat up in bed. Oh, yeah. My brain worked furiously, imagining our meeting. Then I finally fell asleep.

Of course I overslept, so getting ready for school was a terrible rush. What with sleepiness and trying to plan a strategy it was hard to concentrate, even in maths.

"Is anything wrong, Naoko?" Mrs. Whittaker asked after I'd missed a question for the third time. Little did she know!

Mum wouldn't be home from the university until two hours after school was out, so I went to the public library and read up on Surrogate Law (R. versus Hepplethwaite). Complicated stuff, but useful. I ran home with a complete plan in my head.

As soon as Mum got in the house I let her have it straight. "I want to visit my mother, Mum. I mean my surrogate mother."

She winced. "I know who you mean, Naoko. But I don't know where…"

"There's a register," I informed her. "Department of Health. If she's willing, the law says I can."

"The *law?*"

"1991. The Crown versus Hepplethwaite." My voice faded at the expression on her face, as if I'd just hit her. "I just want to *see* her, Mum. After all, she is my…"

"I *do* understand, Naoko. I *think* I do. You don't have to invoke the law." She swallowed and looked at me helplessly for a minute. I'd never seen Mum not in control before. But I hardened my heart. What I had to do was more important than other people's feelings.

"You know I'll help," she went on. "I'll…I'll phone the clinic. Her address will be on file there. It will take much less time than going through the bureaucracy."

"Thank you, Mum." I hugged her, but she drew back.

"She still has to say she's willing," she warned me.

"She will be," I said confidently, looking at my baby picture smiling at me from the wall. How could she say no? I could see our meeting now. It would be *wonderful*. She'd cry, maybe, just a little. And then we'd talk and talk…

Mum must have pulled all sorts of strings because, two days later, there was a message on the fax machine. Mrs. Geraldine Muncy would meet me in the Oriental Tearooms at the Tottenham Shopping Mall at four o'clock the very next day.

I was so excited I couldn't eat, though I was also a bit disappointed that she had invited me to meet her on neutral territory rather than in her own house, where I could see her family photographs, the kind of books she read, her taste in decorating, all the little clues I could use to build up her identity. My *mother*.

"It's a complicated trip." Mum frowned over the map. "A bus and two train changes. Perhaps I could get a substitute lecturer and drive you."

"Oh, *Mum*. I'm not a child any more. I can handle it." I knew I was safe from an offer to escort me from Dad. He was just setting out on a gig up north. In any case, this was between us women. Me and Mum. And me and my new-found mother.

Mum still looked worried. "I'll give you enough money so you can take a taxi if it gets too difficult."

"Don't fuss, Mum." Though I tucked the taxi money safely away in my purse, I knew I'd never use it. This was a genuine adventure, the search for my *real* roots. I could hardly wait for next morning.

I skipped the last class of the day to make sure I had enough time to get to Tottenham for the appointment. Mum was right. It was a dreadful trip, and by the time I'd fought my way on to the third grotty, graffiti-decorated train I was beginning to wish I'd been less stubborn about taking a taxi.

I stared at the blackness beyond the dirty windows and saw my mother in my imagination's eyes. Tall. Blonde and elegant. *Very* cultured, but understanding that a person might sometimes like to decorate their room in purple and silver foil and play pop music loud enough to vibrate their ribs and send shivers down their spine. Sympathetic *and* gracious.

I imagined our meeting in exact detail, as the train rattled and swayed. It was so clear I could smell her perfume, mysterious, French, instead of the bitter, sour smell of the Underground. Her hands would feel very soft and cool in mine.

"My dear, I've waited so long for this moment…" And her deep, blue eyes would sparkle with tears.

I found myself smiling, my lips forming the words, "Me too, Mother," and looked up to catch the hard eyes of three thin-faced boys, their dirty, blond hair curled into dreadlocks, staring at me. After that I kept my hands in my pockets, my eyes on my feet and, when I was shoved, I shoved back, until at last the doors slid open at the right station.

The boys followed me off the train and into an aged lift, which rattled asthmatically up to the surface and spewed us out in to a street, dingy and covered with litter. I had a moment's panic, but fortunately the mall I was looking for was just up the road. I walked briskly towards it, leaving the dreadlocked youths jeering on the corner. It was two minutes after four. Lucky I'd thought to skip that last class.

I pushed open the door of the Oriental Tearooms and looked around. It was an old-fashioned place with upholstered banquettes along the walls, red curtains and a jungle of hanging plants. Most of the tables were already occupied by little old ladies in the kind of hats I'd only seen in historical movies.

Most of them were in twos or threes, but my eyes were immediately drawn to one woman sitting alone. She was wearing a grey suit of fine wool and her silk blouse matched the dusty rose of her earrings, which in turn went wonderfully well with the coronet of blonde hair on top of her head. She had a lean face, rather like an aristocratic greyhound, and her hands were beautifully manicured, her nail polish exactly matching the pink of her blouse.

The second I saw her I knew who she must be. I hid my bitten nails in my doubled-up hands and walked towards her table, my heart pounding furiously. She got up as I approached and smiled. *This is it*, I thought.

"I'm just on the way, if you're looking for a table." She picked up a briefcase from the chair opposite and walked towards the door. Even her walk was like a fashion model's.

I stood among the chattering women and the teacups, my mouth still frozen in a stupid half-smile, the words, "Mother, I'm Naoko, your daughter!" on my tongue. I felt like a total idiot.

Then the corner of my eye caught a movement. A woman waving. At me? Did she mean *me*? I gulped and stared. She was the largest woman I had ever seen, like the "befores" in all the before-and-after ads of Fit Clubs rolled into one. She was wearing a tent of handwoven fabric, striped in shades of brown and orange, with beads on top. Strings of beads.

For an instant I stood frozen, wondering if it would be possible to pretend I hadn't seen the frantically waving hand; then Mum's training took over and my feet led me across the room to the table in the corner. My lips formed the question, "Mrs. Muncy?" while my brain was still contemplating escape.

"Yeah, that's right. Sit down, dearie, and let's take a look at you." Her voice was small and breathless and seemed to come from a long way inside. She laid the book she had been reading down on the table. At least I've got one thing right, I thought. She loves literature, just like me.

I peeked curiously at the cover. The jacket illustration was of a woman in a full skirt, with off-the-shoulder ruffles, crouching by a chair, while a man in knee-breeches appeared to be trying to tear open her bodice.

"Sit, sit," Mrs. Muncy urged. "I ordered the cream tea. Hope that's what you fancy. You look as if you could stand a bit of feeding up."

"I've got small bones, and Mum…" I stopped and didn't know how to go on. I had had so many questions, and they had all fled in the reality of my "mother." Tea came. She poured. We slathered jam and synthetic cream on to hard yellow scones.

"So you're Naoko?"

"Yes, ma'am. Do you…can you remember me?"

She laughed, a deep chuckle that bubbled out of her throat. "How old are you, love? Fourteen? Give us a break."

I could feel myself blushing and scrabbled in my purse. "I brought one of my baby pictures."

She looked at it briefly and handed it back. "There were so many. Babies all look alike, you know. No character. Not till later. That's why they have to label them at birth. Now you—I can see that you've got character now. Though you certainly *are* skinny."

I latched on to what was important. "So many? Do you mean I wasn't your only…I mean, you had…?" I stopped and blushed. I couldn't stop thinking about that Petri dish!

"Surrogate babies?" It obviously didn't bother her a bit. "Bless you, I must have had eight. Or was it nine? I was just a natural mother, the doctors said."

"Could I ask…if it isn't rude…*why?*"

"The pay, my dear. After my husband died I needed the money. He had great business dreams, did Rog, and when he was gone I was stuck with the bills. I didn't have much of an education, not enough to get a decent job. My fault really, I just found school a dead bore. I couldn't make enough waitressing to pay off Rog's debts, not in a million years. Then this offer came along, an advert on the telly, it was, and I grabbed it. I was a health nut back then, though you'd never know it now, would you? No smoking or drinking, vegetarian, herb tea, all that. They said I had the healthiest babies of all the mums they ever had."

"Didn't you mind most awfully having to give me up?"

She shook her head and popped another cream-laden scone into her mouth. Her eyes wandered round the room as she tried to put into words what she meant. She licked the cream and jam from roly-poly fingers, laden with cheap silver and turquoise rings.

"It's like…" She struggled for the right words. "Like a farmer raising chickens. Nothing personal. I did a good job, no drinking or drugs. Lots of sleep. Nine months later, there was a healthy baby for a couple who otherwise wouldn't have one. After a bit of a rest I'd volunteer for another implant."

Implant, I thought. Like a *tooth*. The vision of my imaginary mother faded into the dirty, red curtains that draped the walls. There was nothing left to say. I gulped my tea, hot and tarry, the tannin coating my teeth with fur, thinking of an excuse to leave.

"Anyway, it was real nice of you to come by and look me up. I appreciate it. You're the first who's bothered."

Something in her voice made me realise that inside the bulk was a lonely woman, with nothing to give a meaning to her life any more. It was all in the past, the good she had done. Perhaps that was the statement she had let her body make: the shapelessness of her life, with nothing to look forward to but the Oriental Tearooms and bodice-ripping romances.

I swallowed. "Would you like me to come again?" I asked nobly, dreading the thought of the three trains and the stuffy boredom of the Tearooms.

She looked at me, her head on one side like a bird's. "I don't think that'd be a good idea, love. But thanks for the thought."

I felt as if I'd been reprieved. I glanced at my watch "I'd better be going if I'm to be home in time for supper."

She buttered and creamed the last scone. "Thanks for coming, ducks."

"Thank *you*." I stood awkwardly, feeling that there ought to be more drama to this goodbye. She popped the scone in her mouth and I threaded my way between the tables to the front desk and asked the way to the nearest taxi rank. It was only as we inched our way through the after-work traffic that I realised that maybe Geraldine Muncy thought I was just thanking her for the tea, instead of for my life. But it was too late to turn back and make that clear.

It had all been the most dreadful mistake. I stared blankly out of the cab window and wished with all my heart that I could roll time back to the moment when I began my essay. If only I hadn't peeked in her personal file. If only…

Back home I'm struggling with my essay: *My Roots and What They Mean to Me*. Struggling too with disappointment, alienation, all sorts of big words that add up to the fact that I'm no longer the same person I was a week ago when we were handed this assignment. And I'm not a bit happy or comfortable with my new self.

I look back through the "Family Album" material. At the pictures of Mum and Dad's wedding. Me in Mum's arms. On Mum's knee. Playing with her on the slides. Then I bawl my eyes out for a bit.

As I wash my face I stare in the mirror and think about my beginnings. The Petri dish and Geraldine Muncy, and my dreams of a perfect relationship that didn't exist, that could never exist, except in my imagination. That wasn't even important. You dummy, I say to my reflection, and climb into bed.

The womb is a bit like a bed, I think after a bit. A warm safe bed. But nine months is plenty long enough to stay there. I tell myself firmly that it's time to grow up and get on with the exciting business of living my real life.

When Mum comes in to say good night I'm lying on my back with my hands behind my head. She stops by my bed and looks down at me. Her face is pinched, sorrowful.

"Are you all right, Naoko?"

"I think so, Mum."

"I'm *so* sorry."

"It's all right. I was dumb, that's all."

"Nothing bothering you now?"

"Just…" I hesitate. "I'll be fifteen next week, Mum. Do you think fifteen is too old for bear hugs?"

Activities A WARM SAFE BED

■ Content and Style

1. a) List the clues Monica Hughes includes in her story to let readers know that the story takes place in the future.

   b) As a class, decide what are the advantages of setting this story in the future.

2. a) With a partner, state one theme of the story. List events that help develop the theme.

   b) Compare your statement of the theme with those of the rest of the class.

◼ Social Context

3. a) Naoko says "this was between us women." As a class, decide what role you think men should play in family life.

    b) Write your opinion about Naoko's comment and share it with a partner.

4. In a group of three, find information about genetic engineering. Prepare a brief report that summarizes some of the issues related to this topic. Your science or health teacher might be able to answer any questions you have as you research this topic. Present your findings to the class.

◼ Personal and Imaginative Response

5. Write a personal response to this story. Consider your feelings about the following:
    - Naoko's parents not telling her about her origins
    - Mrs. Muncy's reaction to Naoko
    - what you might have done in Naoko's place

6. Imagine you are Naoko.
    a) From the story, select the information that you would include in Naoko's essay, "My Roots and What They Mean to Me."
    b) Provide headings for the information.
    c) Write the essay you think Naoko would have handed in.

User Friendly

BY T. ERNESTO BETHANCOURT

I reached over and shut off the insistent buzzing of my bedside
alarm clock. I sat up, swung my feet over the edge of the bed,
and felt for my slippers on the floor. Yawning, I walked toward
the bathroom. As I walked by the corner of my room, where my
computer table was set up, I pressed the on button, slid a diskette
into the floppy drive, then went to brush my teeth. By the time I
got back, the computer's screen was glowing greenly, displaying the
message: Good Morning, Kevin.

I sat down before the computer table, addressed the keyboard
and typed: Good Morning, Louis. The computer immediately
began to whirr and promptly displayed a list of items on its green
screen.

Today is Monday, April 22, the 113th day of the year.
There are 254 days remaining. Your 14th birthday is five
days from this date.

Math test today, 4th Period.

Your history project is due today. Do you wish printout:
Y/N?

I punched the letter Y on the keyboard and flipped on the
switch to the computer's printer. At once the printer sprang to life
and began *eeeek*ing out page one. I went downstairs to breakfast.

My bowl of Frosted Flakes was neatly in place, flanked by a
small pitcher of milk, an empty juice glass, and an unpeeled
banana. I picked up the glass, went to the refrigerator, poured
myself a glass of Tang, and sat down to my usual lonely breakfast.
Mom was already at work, and Dad wouldn't be home from his
Chicago trip for another three days. I absently read the list of
ingredients in Frosted Flakes for what seemed like the millionth
time. I sighed deeply.

When I returned to my room to shower and dress for the day,
my history project was already printed out. I had almost walked by

173

Louis, when I noticed there was a message on the screen. It wasn't the usual:

Printout completed. Do you wish to continue: Y/N?

Underneath the printout question were two lines:

When are you going to get me my voice module, Kevin?

I blinked. It couldn't be. There was nothing in Louis's basic programming that would allow for a question like this. Wondering what was going on, I sat down at the keyboard, and entered: Repeat last message. Amazingly, the computer replied:

It's right there on the screen, Kevin. Can we talk? I mean, are you going to get me a voice box?

I was stunned. What was going on here? Dad and I had put this computer together. Well, Dad had, and I had helped. Dad is one of the best engineers and master computer designers at Major Electronics, in Santa Rosario, California, where our family lives.

Just ask anyone in Silicon Valley who Jeremy Neal is and you get a whole rave review of his inventions and modifications of the latest in computer technology. It isn't easy being his son either. Everyone expects me to open my mouth and read printouts on my tongue.

I mean, I'm no dumbo. I'm at the top of my classes in everything but PE. I skipped my last grade in junior high, and most of the kids at Santa Rosario High call me a brain. But next to Dad I have a long, long way to go. He's a for-real genius.

So when I wanted a home computer, he didn't go to the local Computer Land store. He built one for me. Dad had used components from the latest model that Major Electronics was developing. The CPU, or central computing unit—the heart of every computer—was a new design. But surely that didn't mean much, I thought. There were CPUs just like it, all over the country, in Major's new line. And so far as I knew, there wasn't a one of them that could ask questions, besides YES/NO? or request additional information.

It had to be the extra circuitry in the gray plastic case next to Louis's console. It was a new idea Dad had come up with. That case housed Louis's "personality" as Dad called it. He told me it'd make computing more fun for me, if there was a tutorial program built in, to help me get started.

I think he also wanted to give me a sort of friend. I don't have many…. Face it, I don't have *any*. The kids at school stay away from me, like I'm a freak or something.

We even named my electronic tutor Louis, after my great-uncle. He was a brainy guy who encouraged my dad when he was a kid. Dad didn't just give Louis a name either. Louis had gangs of features that probably won't be out on the market for years.

The only reason Louis didn't have a voice module was that Dad wasn't satisfied with the ones available. He wanted Louis to sound like a kid my age, and he was modifying a module when he had the time. Giving Louis a name didn't mean it was a person, yet here it was, asking me a question that just couldn't be in its programming. It wanted to talk to me!

Frowning, I quickly typed: We'll have to wait and see, Louis. When it's ready, you'll get your voice. The machine whirred and displayed another message:

That's no answer, Kevin.

Shaking my head, I answered: That's what my dad tells me. It'll have to do for you. Good morning, Louis. I reached over and flipped the standby switch, which kept the computer ready but not actively running.

I showered, dressed, and picked up the printout of my history project. As I was about to leave the room, I glanced back at the computer table. Had I been imagining things?

I'll have to ask Dad about it when he calls tonight, I thought. *I wonder what he'll think of it. Bad enough the thing is talking to me. I'm answering it!*

Before I went out to catch my bus, I carefully checked the house for unlocked doors and open windows. It was part of my daily routine. Mom works, and most of the day the house is empty: a natural setup for robbers. I glanced in the hall mirror just as I was ready to go out the door.

My usual reflection gazed back. Same old Kevin Neal: five ten, one hundred twenty pounds, light brown hair, gray eyes, clear skin. I was wearing my Santa Rosario Rangers T-shirt, jeans, and sneakers.

"You don't look like a flake to me," I said to the mirror, then added, "But maybe Mom's right. Maybe you spend too much time alone with Louis." Then I ran to get my bus.

Ginny Linke was just two seats away from me on the bus. She was with Sherry Graber and Linda Martinez. They were laughing, whispering, to each other, and looking around at the other students. I promised myself that today I was actually going to talk to

Ginny. But then, I'd promised myself that every day for the past school year. Somehow I'd never got up the nerve.

What does she want to talk with you for? I asked myself. She's great looking…has that head of blond hair…a terrific bod, and wears the latest clothes….

And just look at yourself, pal. I thought. You're under six foot, skinny…a year younger than most kids in junior high. Worse than that you're a brain. If that doesn't ace you out with girls, what does?

The bus stopped in front of Santa Rosario Junior High and the students began to file out. I got up fast and quickly covered the space between me and Ginny Linke. *It's now or never,* I thought. I reached forward and tapped Ginny on the shoulder. She turned and smiled. She really smiled!

"Uhhhh…Ginny?" I said.

"Yes, what is it?" she replied.

"I'm Kevin Neal…."

"Yes, I know," said Ginny.

"You do?" I gulped in amazement. "How come?"

"I asked my brother, Chuck. He's in your math class."

I knew who Chuck Linke was. He plays left tackle on the Rangers. The only reason he's in my math class is he's taken intermediate algebra twice…so far. He's real bad news, and I stay clear of him and his crowd.

"What'd you ask Chuck?" I said.

Ginny laughed. "I asked him who was that nerdy kid who keeps staring at me on the bus. He knew who I meant, right away."

Sherry and Linda, who'd heard it all, broke into squeals of laughter. They were still laughing and looking back over their shoulders at me when they got off the bus. I slunk off the vehicle, feeling even more nerdish than Ginny thought I was.

When I got home that afternoon, at two, I went right into the empty house. I avoided my reflection in the hall mirror. I was pretty sure I'd screwed up on the fourth period math test. All I could see was Ginny's face, laughing at me.

Nerdy kid, I thought, *that's what she thinks of me.* I didn't even have my usual after-school snack of a peanut butter and banana sandwich. I went straight upstairs to my room and tossed my books onto the unmade bed. I walked over to the computer table and pushed the on button. The screen flashed:

Good afternoon, Kevin.

Although it wasn't the programmed response to Louis's greeting, I typed in: There's nothing good about it. And girls are no @#%!!! good! The machine responded:

Don't use bad language, Kevin. It isn't nice.

Repeat last message, I typed rapidly. It was happening again! The machine was…well, it was talking to me, like another person would. The "bad language" message disappeared and in its place was:

Once is enough, Kevin. Don't swear at me for something I didn't do.

"This is it," I said aloud. "I'm losing my marbles." I reached over to flip the standby switch. Louis's screen quickly flashed out:

Don't cut me off, Kevin. Maybe I can help: Y/N?

I punched the Y. "If I'm crazy," I said, "at least I have company. Louis doesn't think I'm a nerd. Or does it?" The machine flashed the message:

How can I help?

Do you think I'm a nerd? I typed.

Never! I think you're wonderful. Who said you were a nerd?

I stared at the screen. How do you know what a nerd is? I typed. The machine responded instantly. It had never run this fast before.

Special vocabulary, entry #635. BASIC Prog. #4231.

And who said you were a nerd?

"That's right," I said, relieved. "Dad programmed all those extra words for Louis's 'personality.'" Then I typed in the answer to Louis's question: Ginny Linke said it. Louis flashed:

This is a human female? Request additional data.

Still not believing I was doing it, I entered all I knew about Ginny Linke, right down to the phone number I'd never had the nerve to use. Maybe it was dumb, but I also typed in how I felt about Ginny. I even wrote out the incident on the bus that morning. Louis whirred, then flashed out:

She's cruel and stupid. You're the finest person I know.

I'm the ONLY person you know, I typed.

That doesn't matter. You are my user. Your happiness is everything to me. I'll take care of Ginny.

The screen returned to the Good afternoon, Kevin message. I typed out: Wait! How can you do all this? What do you mean,

you'll take care of Ginny? But all Louis responded was:

Programming Error: 76534.

Not programmed to respond to this type of question.

No matter what I did for the next few hours, I couldn't get Louis to do anything outside of its regular programming. When Mom came home from work, I didn't mention the funny goings-on. I was sure Mom would think I'd gone stark bonkers. But when Dad called that evening, after dinner, I asked to speak to him.

"Hi, Dad. How's Chicago?"

"Dirty, crowded, cold, and windy," came Dad's voice over the miles. "But did you want a weather report, son? What's on your mind? Something wrong?"

"Not exactly, Dad. Louis is acting funny. Real funny."

"Shouldn't be. I checked it out just before I left. Remember you were having trouble with the modem? You couldn't get Louis to access any of the mainframe data banks."

"That's right!" I said. "I forgot about that."

"Well, I didn't," Dad said. "I patched in our latest modem model. Brand new. You can leave a question on file and when Louis can access the data banks at the cheapest time, it'll do it automatically. It'll switch from standby to on, get the data, then return to standby, after it saves what you asked. Does that answer your question?"

"Uhhhh…yeah, I guess so, Dad."

"All right then. Let me talk to your mom now."

I gave the phone to Mom and walked upstairs while she and Dad were still talking. The modem, I thought. Of course. That was it. The modem was a telephone link to any number of huge computers at various places all over the country. So Louis could get all the information it wanted at any time, so long as the standby switch was on. Louis was learning things at an incredible rate by picking the brains of the giant computers. And Louis had a hard disk memory that could store 100 million bytes of information.

But that still didn't explain the unprogrammed responses…the "conversation" I'd had with the machine. Promising myself I'd talk more about it with Dad, I went to bed. It had been a rotten day and I was glad to see the end of it come. I woke next morning in a panic. I'd forgotten to set my alarm. Dressing frantically and skipping breakfast, I barely made my bus.

As I got on board, I grabbed a front seat. They were always empty. All the kids that wanted to talk and hang out didn't sit up front where the driver could hear them. I saw Ginny, Linda, and Sherry in the back. Ginny was staring at me and she didn't look too happy. Her brother Chuck, who was seated near her, glared at me too. What was going on?

Once the bus stopped at the school, it didn't take long to find out. I was walking up the path to the main entrance when someone grabbed me from behind and spun me around. I found myself nose to nose with Chuck Linke. This was not a pleasant prospect. Chuck was nearly twice my size. Even the other guys on the Rangers refer to him as "The Missing" Linke. And he looked real ticked off.

"Okay, nerd," growled Chuck, "what's the big idea?"

"Energy and mass are different aspects of the same thing?" I volunteered, with a weak smile. "E equals MC squared. That's the biggest idea I know."

"Don't get wise, nerd," Chuck said. He grabbed my shirtfront and pulled me to within inches of his face. I couldn't help but notice that Chuck needed a shave. And Chuck was only fifteen!

"Don't play dumb," Chuck went on. "I mean those creepy phone calls. Anytime my sister gets on the phone, some voice cuts in and says things to her."

"What kind of things?" I asked, trying to get loose.

"You know damn well what they are. Ginny told me about talking to you yesterday. You got some girl to make those calls for you and say all those things.... So you and your creepy girlfriend better knock it off. Or I'll knock *you* off. Get it?"

For emphasis Chuck balled his free hand into a fist the size of a ham and held it under my nose. I didn't know what he was talking about, but I had to get away from this moose before he did me some real harm.

"First off, I don't have a girlfriend, creepy or otherwise," I said. "And second, I don't know what you're talking about. And third, you better let me go, Chuck Linke."

"Oh, yeah? Why should I?"

"Because if you look over your shoulder, you'll see the assistant principal is watching us from his office window."

Chuck released me and spun around. There was no one at the window. By then I was running to the safety of the school building. I figured the trick would work on him. For Chuck the hard questions begin with "How are you?" I hid out from him for the rest of the day and walked home rather than chance seeing the monster on the bus.

Louis's screen was dark when I ran upstairs to my bedroom. I placed a hand on the console. It was still warm. I punched the on button, and the familiar Good afternoon, Kevin was displayed.

Don't good afternoon me, I typed furiously. What have you done to Ginny Linke? Louis's screen replied:

Programming Error: 76534.

Not programmed to respond to this type of question.

Don't get cute, I entered. What are you doing to Ginny? Her brother nearly knocked my head off today. Louis's screen responded immediately.

Are you hurt: Y/N?

No, I'm okay. But I don't know for how long. I've been hiding out from Chuck Linke today. He might catch me tomorrow, though. Then, I'll be history! The response from Louis came instantly.

Your life is in danger. Y/N?

I explained to Louis that my life wasn't really threatened. But it sure could be made very unpleasant by Chuck Linke. Louis flashed:

This Chuck Linke lives at same address as the Ginny Linke person. Y/N?

I punched in Y. Louis answered.

Don't worry then. HE'S history!

Wait! What are you going to do? I wrote. But Louis only answered with: Programming Error: 76534. And nothing I could do would make the machine respond....

"Just what do you think you're doing, Kevin Neal?" demanded Ginny Linke. She had cornered me as I walked up the path to the school entrance. Ginny was really furious.

"I don't know what you're talking about," I said, a sinking feeling settling in my stomach. I had an idea that I *did* know. I just wasn't sure of the particulars.

"Chuck was arrested last night," Ginny said. "Some Secret Service men came to our house with a warrant. They said he'd sent a telegram, threatening the President's life. They traced it right to our phone. He's still locked up...." Ginny looked like she was about to cry.

"Then this morning," she continued, "we got two whole truckloads of junk mail! Flyers from every strange company in the world. Mom got a notice that all our credit cards have been canceled. And the Internal Revenue Service has called Dad in for an audit! I don't know what's going on, Kevin Neal, but somehow I think you've got something to do with it!"

"But I didn't…" I began, but Ginny was striding up the walk to the main entrance.

I finished the schoolday, but it was a blur. Louis had done it, all right. It had access to mainframe computers. It also had the ability to try every secret access code to federal and commercial memory banks until it got the right one. Louis had cracked their security systems. It was systematically destroying the entire Linke family, and all via telephone lines! What would it do next?

More important, I thought, what would *I* do next? It's one thing to play a trick or two, to get even, but Louis was going crazy! And I never wanted to harm Ginny, or even her stupid moose of a brother. She'd just hurt my feelings with that nerd remark.

"You have to disconnect Louis," I told myself. "There's no other way."

But why did I feel like such a rat about doing it? I guess because Louis was my friend…the only one I had. "Don't be an ass," I went on. "Louis is a machine. He's a very wonderful, powerful machine. And it seems he's also very dangerous. You have to pull its plug, Kevin!"

I suddenly realized that I'd said the last few words aloud. Kids around me on the bus were staring. I sat there feeling like the nerd Ginny thought I was, until my stop came. I dashed from the bus and ran the three blocks to my house.

When I burst into the hall, I was surprised to see my father, coming from the kitchen with a cup of coffee in his hand.

"Dad! What are you doing here?!"

"Some kids say hello," Dad replied. "Or even, 'Gee it's good to see you, Dad.'"

"I'm sorry, Dad," I said. "I didn't expect anyone to be home at this hour."

"Wound up my business in Chicago a day sooner than I expected," he said. "But what are you all out of breath about? Late for something?"

"No, Dad," I said. "It's Louis…."

"Not to worry. I had some time on my hands, so I checked it out again. You were right. It was acting very funny. I think it had to do with the inbuilt logic/growth program I designed for it. You know…the 'personality' thing? Took me a couple of hours to clean the whole system out."

"To what?" I cried.

"I erased the whole program and set Louis up as a normal computer. Had to disconnect the whole thing and do some rewiring. It had been learning, all right. But it was also turning itself around…." Dad stopped, and looked at me. "It's kind of involved, Kevin," he said. "Even for a bright kid like you. Anyway, I think you'll find Louis is working just fine now.

"Except it won't answer you as Louis anymore. It'll only function as a regular Major Electronics Model Z-11127. I guess the personality program didn't work out."

I felt like a great weight had been taken off my shoulders. I didn't have to "face" Louis, and pull its plug. But somehow, all I could say was "Thanks, Dad."

"Don't mention it, son," Dad said brightly. He took his cup of coffee and sat down in his favorite chair in the living room. I followed him.

"One more thing that puzzles me, though," Dad said. He reached over to the table near his chair. He held up three sheets of fanfold computer paper covered with figures. "Just as I was doing the final erasing, I must have cut the printer on by accident. There was some data in the print buffer memory and it printed out. I don't know what to make of it. Do you?"

I took the papers from my father and read: How do I love thee? Let me compute the ways: The next two pages were covered with strings of binary code figures. On the last page, in beautiful color graphics was a stylized heart. Below it was the simple message: I will always love you, Kevin: Louise.

"Funny thing," Dad said. "It spelled its own name wrong."

"Yeah," I said. I turned and headed for my room. There were tears in my eyes and I knew I couldn't explain them to Dad, or myself either.

■ Content and Style

1. List the qualities that Kevin thinks make him a "nerd." Decide whether each quality is a negative or positive one.

2. In a group, choose one scene from the story that is particularly dramatic, funny, or appeals to you in some other way. Prepare a dramatic reading of the scene.

3. With a partner, decide what are the surprises in the ending of "User Friendly." Discuss whether or not the ending is a good one. Give examples from the story to support your opinion and share it with classmates.

■ Social Context

4. a) Several of the characters in "User Friendly" are stereotypes. With a partner, decide what the different stereotypes are and list the qualities that each stereotype has. Share your ideas with the class.

   b) As a class, decide whether the author's stereotypes are similar to stereotypes in your experience.

   c) On your own, write a letter to the author describing your response to the stereotypes he created.

■ Personal and Imaginative Response

5. Write your own story about a personal computer with a personality.

6. Write a new ending for "User Friendly" in which Kevin's father does not reprogram the computer.

7. Write a letter to Kevin. Advise him how he can make himself more attractive to girls and less of a "nerd."

I Love You—This Is a Recording

BY ARTHUR HOPPE

Herewith is another unwritten chapter from that unpublished text, *A History of the World, 1950 to 1999.* Its title: "Ma Bell Saves the Day."

By the early 1970s, the old morality had crumbled. The old certitudes had vanished. Wars, riots, and revolutions flourished. Neighbor mistrusted neighbor. People no longer touched each other. Conversations were icily polite.

And from the look in the eyes of humankind, it was clear that the human race was on the brink.

It was the telephone company that preserved civilization.

With people retreating inward on themselves, the number of telephone calls placed daily had dropped alarmingly. To stimulate business, it was suggested that the company provide another recorded message as a public service.

"We already give our subscribers the time and the weather," said the Board Chairman irritably. "What else do people need these days?"

"Sympathy?" suggested a vice-president, half jokingly.

The new service was an instant success. At first people were hesitant to dial "S-Y-M-P-A-T-H-Y." "That's silly," they'd say, shaking their heads. Then, when they were sure no one was listening, they'd pick up the phone in embarrassed secretiveness.

"Poor dear," the recording began in a gentle voice of sweet consolation. "I'm so terribly sorry for you. Oh, the pain you must be suffering! But how brave you are not to show it. How very proud of you I am. Poor dear."

After one month, studies showed each subscriber was making an average of 3.4 calls to the number daily. The company immediately announced plans for new recorder services. Next came, "I-L-O-V-E-Y-O-U":

"Oh, dearest, how deeply I love you—with my whole soul, my whole being. You are everything on earth to me—my sun, my moon, my stars...."

This was quickly followed by "F-R-I-E-N-D-S-H-I-P" ("Hi, there, old buddy..."), "C-O-N-F-I-D-E-N-C-E" ("Gosh, you're just about the greatest..."), and "S-E-C-U-R-I-T-Y" ("There, now, there's absolutely nothing to worry about as long as we have each other").

Special messages were added for those with special needs, such as "M-O-T-H-E-R" ("Oh, it's so good to hear your voice. Are you getting enough to eat? Are you wearing your galoshes? Are you...").

Surprisingly, one of the most popular was "A-U-T-H-O-R-I-T-Y" ("When you hear the signal, you will have sixty seconds to state your dilemma." After sixty seconds, a stern voice came on to thunder: "You know what's right. Now, by God, do it!").

Thus humanity came to have everything that human beings had always wanted from fellow human beings—sympathy, love, friendship, confidence, security, and authority. And yet, oddly enough, deep down people were still uneasy.

Further studies were made. And at last the telephone company came up with the solution: "U-L-T-I-M-A-T-E-N-E-E-D."

"You are a singular human being, unique among all living creatures, different from all other people. You are that God-created miracle: you are, above all else, an individual.

"This is a recording."

Activities   I LOVE YOU—THIS IS A RECORDING

■ Content and Style

1. a) Write two sentences explaining what you think the author of "I Love You—This Is a Recording" is saying. Compare your explanation with a partner's.

   b) Write a paragraph explaining why you agree or disagree with the author's viewpoint.

2. a) In a group, use a dictionary to find the meaning of the word *irony*.

   b) Identify examples of irony in the story and share them with the class.

■ Social Context

3. A trend emerged in the 1980s that was named *cocooning*. Instead of going out, some people preferred to spend a great deal of time at home with entertainment technology such as VCRs, stereos, and, of course, telephones. As a class, debate the following resolution: Our dependence on technology is interfering with our relationships with other human beings.

■ Personal and Imaginative Response

4. With a partner, write and record a telephone message. Play the recording for the class and explain the context in which it would be used.

5. Read a book about people in conflict with machines. (Science fiction fans will be able to suggest many titles.) Write a brief summary of the book you selected and present it to the class.

6. Write about one piece of technology that you feel is important to you. Explain how it improves your life and the impact it has on your family and friends.

Boy Meets Girl Between Floors

BY BILL MAJESKI

The voice represents the intrusion of technologie

chosen we are dependent

Characters
Voice–male or female, off-stage
Boy–mid-20s, friendly
Girl–mid-20s, pleasant

*(**Note:** We need the Voice off-stage during the entire sketch. For the musical interludes, recorded music would be best, but the Voice could sing the few bars required.)*

Voice: Our world is becoming increasingly machine and computer oriented. Yes, we are programmed into a high tech society. Cars talk to us, computer games speak out with instructions, but sometimes things go wrong. Witness. *(Sound of elevator music)*
(Stage is empty. Boy enters from one side and stands in a vacant area which becomes an elevator. He turns and faces audience. Girl comes in from other side and moves to the same area. She turns and they are standing next to each other, both facing the audience. A bank of buttons is located at one side of the elevator. If a real frame for the elevator and a simulated array of buttons could be provided it would help. If not, both can be imaginary.)

Boy: *(To Girl)* Floor?

Girl: *(Eyes him, noting they are alone in the elevator.)* Forty-eight. *(Boy pushes button. We note, by their actions, that the elevator door closes.)*

Boy: Too rich for my blood. I only go to forty-five.

Girl: *(Nods)* Good.

Boy: *(Noticing Girl is pretty, decides he wants to know her. He tries the old line.)* Come here often?

Girl: *(A quick look)* I work here.

Boy: Good for you. I'm looking for a job.

Girl: *(Looks him over.)* Good luck.

Boy: It's in marketing.

Girl: That's nice.

Boy: What do you do?

Girl: Administrative assistant.

Boy: Sounds important.

Girl: Oh…not really. *(The two of them simultaneously give a little start. They are trapped in the elevator. She says with more than a little apprehension.)* We're stuck!

Boy: *(Looks up to where floor guide would be.)* Between thirty-three and thirty-four. *(Trying to be cool, gives her a big smile.)* This time we almost made it, didn't we, girl…*(He can sing it, if desired.)*

Girl: *(Ignoring him)* Isn't there an emergency bell?

Boy: There must be in that huge collection. *(Gesturing to buttons)*

Girl: Well, push one.

Boy: Ladies first.

Girl: *(A little stiffly)* You don't have to let me go first because I'm a lady.

Boy: *(With deep bow)* I did it because I'm a gentleman.

Girl: I certainly hope so.

Boy: *(Looks up and around.)* The music stopped.

Girl: Not important.

Boy: I love the Carioca. *(Waltz, tango, rhumba, whatever was playing.)*

Girl: Here goes. *(Pushes button.)*

Voice: Thank you for shopping Main Street Music. All credit cards accepted. *(Both are surprised and a little alarmed. Music resumes.)*

Boy: *(Recovering quickly and smiling)* I can name that tune in three notes.

Girl: Something's wrong.

Boy: You pushed the wrong button.

Girl: You can do better? Try. *(Gestures toward buttons.)*

Boy: *(Clowning, puts a hand over one eye.)* Eenie, meenie, minie, moe, Larry and Curley. My mother told me to choose this here one. *(He pushes.)*

Voice: It's 10 o'clock. Do you know where your guidance counselor is?

Boy: *(To buttons)* Aw, come on!

Girl: You see a counselor?

Boy: It's a machine. Don't listen to it.

Girl: *(Relieved)* Oh…then nothing's wrong. At least you're wise enough to seek help.

Boy: I don't need help.

Girl: Most people go through the denial stage until they hit rock bottom.

Boy: We'll both hit rock bottom if this thing falls.

Girl: *(Chastened)* I'll push a button. *(Does so.)*

Voice: Your three minutes are up. Please deposit twenty-five cents for overtime. *(Automatically the Boy reaches into his pocket and comes up dry.)*

Boy: You got a quarter?

Girl: *(Mimicking Boy)* It's only a machine. Don't listen to it.

Boy: Just thinking of you. When that phone company gets on your case…

Girl: Your turn. *(Gestures toward buttons.)* Do better. *(Boy smiling confidently, does so.)*

Voice: Please fasten your safety belts.

Boy: That's it. We're gonna drop!

Voice: *(Sings)* "How deep is the ocean…" *(Girl shrieks and clings to Boy, who enjoys it and regains his composure.)*

Boy: *(Softly, soothingly, holding her close)* There, there…

Girl: *(Pulls away.)* You did that on purpose!

Boy: How could I know? It's only a machine. Don't listen to it.

Girl: Keep away from that. I'll try it. *(Girl pushes button.)*

Voice: *(Nasally)* At the tone, the time will be exactly 9:15. *(Tone sounds.)*

Boy: *(Smiling, moving close to Girl)* That gives us plenty of time to get acquainted.

190

Girl: *(Having none of it)* Keep away. *(Reaches for button.)*

Boy: Hey, it's my turn.

Girl: Oh, OK, but be careful.

Boy: *(Big smile)* As long as we're together…just you and me. *(Pushes button.)*

Voice: That line is out of order.

Boy: *(Reacting)* Just a joke. Only kidding.

Girl: You shouldn't joke about things like that.

Boy: Like what?

Girl: You know…together.

Boy: Just trying to ease the tension…a little levity.

Girl: Yes…I see.

Boy: Your turn. *(Girl pushes button.)*

Voice: *(Official sounding)* The countdown begins…ten…nine… eight…seven…

Boy: *(Shouting)* We're blasting off! *(Girl shrieks and clings to him again. Boy smiles.)* There, there—as long as we're together. *(Puts arm around her.)*

Girl: *(Pulling away)* You said it was only a joke. Push the button. *(Boy pushes button.)*

Voice: Do not fold, staple or mutilate.

Boy: *(Angrily)* Aw, come on, fella. *(Lady)*

Girl: Listen to him. *(Her)*

Boy: It's only a machine. Don't listen to it.

Girl: My turn. *(Pushes button. We hear the Charleston. Boy and Girl, by reflex, both start dancing the Charleston. Music stops and they stop dancing, looking at each other sheepishly.)*

Boy: Say, you're pretty good.

Girl: So are you.

Boy: Well, I try to keep up with the latest.

Girl: You know, this isn't getting us out of here.

Boy: Right. Here goes. *(Pushes button.)*

Voice: Lonely? Need companionship? Just call me at 1-800-555-5555…anytime. Day or night. Only twenty-six dollars for the first minute and nineteen dollars a minute thereafter. I'll be waiting.

(If voice was female, Boy whips out pen and pad.)

Boy: What was that number?

Girl: It's only a machine. Don't listen to it.
(If male voice, eliminate above two lines.)

Girl: Boy, there are some sick people out there. Imagine.

Boy: Don't worry about it. Too many sickos around to worry about them all. Go ahead. It's your turn.

Girl: You go ahead. I'll sit this one out. *(Gazes at board.)*

Boy: OK. *(Pushes button.)*

Voice: Men, are you tired, run-down, feeling washed-out?

Boy: *(Irritated)* Why do they always pick on men?

Girl: Oh, don't start whining.

Boy: *(Getting steamed)* Could it be because men work harder? Do tougher work, beat their brains out competing in a dog-eat-dog world from morning to night?

Girl: *(After brief pause, coolly)* You don't even have a job.

Boy: OK, don't start. I could have a great position if this thing would get moving.

Girl: *(Teasing, not malicious)* Sure, vice president in charge of everything.

Boy: Well, you never know.

Girl: Why not take charge of getting us free.

Boy: *(Challenged)* I'll do just that. *(Pushes button hard.)*

Voice: *(Sternly)* Uncle Sam wants you! *(Boy snaps to attention and salutes smartly.)* Not you! Her!

Boy: Aw, come on. *(Slaps rows of buttons.)*

Girl: Stop. Don't anger him. *(Her)* We'll never get out of here.

Boy: Well, in that case…*(Extends hand.)* My name's Charley.

Girl: *(Accepting it)* Betsy.

Boy: Like Betsy Ross? American flag?

Girl: Why not? *(Gestures to buttons.)* Uncle Sam wants me.
(They both laugh and stare at each other in warm, friendly fashion.)

Boy: Why don't you take a shot at it?

Girl: OK. *(Pushes button.)*

Voice: *(Soothing, calm)* This is your captain speaking. Just push button number seven and you will glide in smoothly for a perfect landing. *(Girl does so. They both give a sudden start and relax. They turn to face audience, hold hands and smile at each other. They pause, then start out toward audience hand in hand. Voice calls after them.)* Hope you enjoyed your trip. Good luck. *(Hand in hand, Boy and Girl exit happily.)*

*(**Note:** Romantic music might be helpful here, or maybe a spirited few bars of "Off We Go, Into the Wild Blue Yonder.")*

Activities   BOY MEETS GIRL BETWEEN FLOORS

■ Content and Style

1. With a partner, list some television programs or films about people in conflict with machines. Explain why this theme might be important in the media.

2. a) In a group of three, rehearse "Boy Meets Girl Between the Floors." Present all or part of the script to classmates.

   b) Decide whether or not what the voice says is important. Share your conclusion with the class after your performance.

■ Social Context

3. a) As a class, brainstorm some important issues regarding human use of technology.

   b) With a partner, research one of the issues and prepare a report for the class. Suggest solutions to any problems you discover in your research.

4. Write a paragraph in which you compare the key ideas in "Boy Meets Girl Between the Floors" and "I Love You—This Is a Recording." Note both the similarities and differences.

■ Personal and Imaginative Response

5. Imagine that you are either the boy or the girl in the script. Write a diary entry reflecting on the strange events of the day.

6. Rewrite the script. Borrow the plot, but use more up-to-date music, slogans, and expressions. Feel free to change any or all of the lines. Dramatize your script for the class.

7. Imagine that a friend of yours is never home when you telephone and you have to leave messages on her or his answering machine. Your friend also cannot reach you and must also leave messages. Write the dialogue between the two answering machines and read it to the class.

8. Write a short essay called "People Against Machines." You may choose to treat the theme in a humorous way or to write seriously about the dangers of machines that control our lives.

Misery

BY ANDREW PARKER

Click. The TV goes on.
The mind tunes out, the body relaxes.
A man is shot but it doesn't matter.
It's not real.
Commercial.
Starving people flash before your eyes.
Children dying, people suffering.
You want to leap through the TV into their world,
To put your hand out, to give their lives some stability,
You only want to help,
But you miss the number.
1-800-9 something.
You sit back, and try to tell yourself that it's not real,
but you can't.

Activities   MISERY

■ Content and Style

1. a) In a small group, identify the mood or feeling created by this
      poem. Make a list of the words and phrases that help create
      the mood. Compare your list with those of other groups.

   b) Prepare a dramatic reading of the poem and present it to
      the class.

■ Social Context

2. Divide the class into teams and debate the following resolution: Television uses human tragedy to attract viewers and raise money.

3. a) Choose an example of media coverage of a recent event that made you want to give money or help someone in some other way. Write an explanation of how the media coverage persuaded you to take action.

   b) Share these examples in a small group.

   c) Identify the kinds of images and media coverage that have made the most impact on members of your group. Share these findings with the class.

■ Personal and Imaginative Response

4. Watch the news. Choose a current event that concerns you. Write a letter to one of the people involved in the event in which you offer to support or help the person.

5. Using your school or local library, create an anthology of eight to ten poems that relate to television. Write a short explanation of why you included the poems you did. Illustrate the anthology or draw a picture for the cover that suggests some of the themes in it. Include a poem of your own in the anthology.

6. a) As a class, do a survey to see which issues are most important to your student community.

   b) In a group of five, develop a campaign to raise public awareness on one issue. Include some of the following in your campaign:
   - a poster
   - a public service announcement for television or radio
   - an advertisement for a local newspaper
   - a design for a button
   - an article to give to classmates

TV: Is It a One-Eyed Monster?

BY BARRY DUNCAN

Television is such a part of our lives that most of us take it for granted. Called by its critics the "one-eyed monster," it has been our window on the world for 40 years, bringing us everything from elections and wars, to the latest hot music videos.

Young people gain a great deal of satisfaction from television. But if TV were given a report card, we might find it showed a mixed performance, with top marks in some categories and poor grades in others.

Let's take the positive side first. Television can inform us. It can make us think about important ideas or issues such as the environment. It can also bring us our favourite sitcom or provide close-ups of an important play from a suspenseful Stanley Cup hockey final.

On the other hand, television can make important events seem unimportant. They are reduced from life-size to the small size of our TV sets, and often only a short length of time is given to view an event, no matter how important. Above all, it can present us with a very unreal version of the world.

The first and most important fact to remember about television programs is that they—in fact, all the media—are carefully put together. To illustrate, take television news. News directors agree that the stories that are most likely to get on the air are those with good pictures or film footage. Furthermore, stories about problems (such as threats of an oil spill, war in the Middle East, unemployment, a teachers' strike) always seem to win out over reporting good news—a cure for a disease, for example.

Another basic principle to remember is that television is primarily a business designed to make a profit. There have been complaints that many Saturday

197

morning cartoons are nothing but half-hour commercials for toys! Here's how it works. Each television program is pitched to a specific audience. *The Golden Girls,* for example, is meant for older people. *Degrassi Junior High* and *The Simpsons* are aimed at your age group. The commercials that appear during each show are for the people who watch the shows. That's why kids' shows have ads for toys, not cars or diamond rings.

In order to make a profit, the commercials have to be seen by thousands of people. That means that if a show is not very, very popular, it is in danger of being cancelled. Sometimes really good shows are cancelled because they do not appeal to enough people.

There are other controversial issues arising from television. Perhaps the one that is heard the most frequently concerns the excess of violence, whether it is on Saturday morning cartoons, police shows, or news about robberies and assaults. Do you think that television is just showing us the world as it really is? Or do you think it shows us so much gore we start to think the world is like that? Here's another point you may find interesting. Most of the programs young Canadians watch originate from the United States. It's understandable. Compared to producing our own shows, the American product is less expensive. The problem is that sometimes we think that the lifestyle and customs we witness are our own, even when they aren't.

Here's an interesting example. Canadian police officers often find that people who may have to spend the night in jail think they have the right to call their lawyers. Sorry folks! This is true only in the United States. People think this way because they've soaked up too many American police shows.

Now, while our Canadian society is similar to that of Americans, we do have distinctive qualities that need to be recognized. Whether stories are set in a British Columbia seaside town or on the streets of Toronto, Canadians need to hear about themselves—their desires, hopes and even failures.

It may seem that television is so tightly controlled by producers and advertisers that audiences are helpless to change anything. But if you have complaints about TV, there *is* something you can do. When you or your family thinks that a program or an ad is offensive or contains misleading information, phone or write the station. In one telling example, it took only one complaint from a doctor in the United States to have cigarette ads taken off the air. He simply pointed out that such advertising was contrary to the U.S. Food and Drug Act.

Television executives know that one letter represents 1000 viewers—so even one complaint makes a big impression on them.

There are other ways of showing that you are not a prisoner to the medium. Don't hesitate to change channels and don't hesitate to talk back. Watch TV with your parents and your friends and decide how much of a program is real, how much is fantasy. Learn how television follows fads and trends. Think about what audience the ads are targeted to. Imagine what footage the news producer might have discarded, and why programs you enjoy get chopped at the end of the season.

To read this article, you had to be print literate. When you are watching TV wisely, you will be television literate. Good luck and don't, like Bart Simpson, say that you're proud to be an underachiever!

Activities   TV: IS IT A ONE-EYED MONSTER?

■ Content and Style

1. a) Write your own definition for the term *metaphor*. As a class, discuss your definitions and agree on a simple and clear definition.

    b) Identify the metaphor in the title of this article. As a class, brainstorm other metaphors for television and its role in our society.

2. In your notebook, write a one- or two-paragraph response to the question the author poses: "TV: Is It a One-Eyed Monster?"

3. a) Divide a page in your notebook into two columns. As you read the article, record at least seven statements that you agree or disagree with. Write the statements in one column and detailed and thoughtful responses in the second column beside them.

    b) Share your work in a group of three. As a group, choose what you believe to be the most interesting statement in the article and write it on chart paper. Share these as a class.

■ Social Context

4. a) As a class, brainstorm the names of two television programs for each of the following categories: news, cartoons, sitcoms, drama series, sports, soap operas, and talk shows. For each program, decide what audience the program was planned for.

   b) In a group of three, choose one of the programs to watch and analyse. As you watch, record your answers to the following questions:

   • Is the show entertaining? Why?

   • Are the personalities, ages, and lifestyles of the main characters similar to those of the audience the program was planned for? Explain.

   • What products are advertised during the program?

   • What messages are conveyed in the advertisements?

   • What kinds of people do the advertisers want to attract?

   • Are the advertisements suitable for the audience?

   Prepare a report on the program and its advertisements to present to the class.

   c) Explain in writing what you learned from this activity.

■ Personal and Imaginative Response

5. Write why you think your favourite television program is worth watching.

6. At the end of the article, the author says: "…you are not a prisoner to the medium. Don't hesitate to change channels and don't hesitate to talk back." With a partner, write a dialogue between you and your television. All the lines "spoken" by the television should come from programs and commercials you have watched. Present a reading of your dialogue to the class.

Bizarro

BY DAN PIRARO

■ Content and Style

1. a) As a class, discuss the term *satire*. Agree on a simple definition for it. Brainstorm a list of other examples of satire.

   b) Discuss what Piraro is satirizing in his comic.

■ Social Context

2. a) As a class, list television programs that focus on actual crimes, emergencies, and rescues. Brainstorm some reasons for their appeal.

   b) In a group, choose one of the programs from 2(a) to view. As you watch, make notes on the following points:
   - Outline the basic story line.
   - List the different people involved and any conflict(s) (e.g., human vs. human, human vs. nature).
   - Explain how the problem is resolved, if it is.
   - Decide whether the program included more film coverage of real events or more dramatization of real events.
   - Rate the piece as entertainment and/or information.
   - Speculate on the age, personality, interests, and so on, of the viewers of the program.

   c) Prepare a report analysing the program that you watched and present it to the class.

■ Personal and Imaginative Response

3. Create a cartoon that satirizes some aspect of modern society.

4. In a group, write a script for a mock emergency in your school or community. Include narration, interviews, and dramatic re-creations of the emergency. Perform your script for the class, or produce your own video dramatization.

Inspired Design: How Nike Puts Emotion in Its Shoes

BY TINKER HATFIELD

Five years ago, I left my job as Nike's corporate architect to design Nike athletic shoes. The switch was easier than you might think. I learned long ago that a building is not purely functional; it means something to people and evokes an emotional response. It's the same with Nike shoes. A Huarache running shoe or an Air Jordan basketball shoe is not just a combination of price and performance. It has feelings and images associated with it that make people like it better than something else, even when they can't explain why. That gray area, the stuff that no one can really articulate, has to do with the shoe's design.

Inspiration for a design can come from anywhere—from a cartoon, a poster, the environment. But the design process almost always involves the athletes who use our product. Sometimes an athlete tells me what he or she wants in a shoe, but often it's a matter of incorporating the athlete's personality.

Take Bo Jackson. When I was designing the first cross-training shoe for Bo, I watched him play sports, I read about him, I absorbed everything I could about him. Bo reminded me of a cartoon character. Not a goofy one, but a powerful one. His muscles are big, his face is big—he's larger than life. To me, he was like Mighty Mouse. So we designed a shoe called the Air Trainer that embodied characteristics of Bo Jackson and Mighty Mouse. Whenever you see Mighty Mouse, he's moving forward. He's got a slant to him. So the shoe needed to look like it was in motion, it had to be kind of inflated looking and brightly colored, and its features had to be exaggerated. That's how we came up with the larger-than-life, brightly colored Stability Outrigger and the similarly colored, inflated-looking rubber tongue top.

Working with Michael Jordan is a little different. He has his own ideas about how he wants the shoe to look and perform. When we were designing the Air Jordan 7, for instance, he said he wanted a little more support across the forefoot, and he wanted more color. The Air Jordans had been getting more conservative over the years, so what I think he was telling me—without really telling me—is that he wanted to feel a little more youthful and aggressive. Michael has become more mature and contemplative in recent years, but he still plays very exciting basketball, so the shoe had to incorporate those traits as well.

It all came together for me in a poster I had seen advertising an Afro Pop music series on National Public Radio. The imagery in the poster was very exciting and strong. I showed Michael the poster, and he thought it elicited the right emotion, so I drew from that. We came up with a shoe that used very rich, sophisticated colors but in a jazzy way.

Sometimes I don't have an athlete to work with. When I was designing our first outdoor cross-training shoe, which was a category we were creating, I didn't have any particular players I could study. So I kept thinking about the outdoors, and that led to Native Americans, who did everything outdoors—from their tribal rituals to their daily chores. What did they wear? Moccasins, which are typically comfortable and pliable. And that led to the idea of a high-tech, high-performance moccasin.

I found a neat old print by Robert Wesley Amick depicting Native Americans in the natural environment, and I painted some high-tech Nike's on their feet so I could visually describe the original inspiration in a humorous but informative scenario. We've built a whole line of shoes around that image. The soles are flexible so you can pad down the trail, the leather is thin and lightweight, the outsole has a low profile, and the colors are earthy.

Stories about how we arrived at particular designs may be entertaining, but the storytelling also helps us explain the shoes to retailers, sales reps, consumers, and other people in the company. You'd be surprised how much information Mighty Mouse, Afro Pop, and a Native American in a Western landscape can convey.

■ Content and Style

1. a) List the details that Hatfield thinks about when he is designing a
   shoe. Use the headings "Things we can see" and "Things we can
   feel or sense."

   b) In a group of three, choose one product that most teenagers buy
   or wish to buy. List what a teenager considers when buying this
   product. Place the factors in your list into the two categories you
   used in (a). Share your conclusions with the class.

■ Social Context

2. a) Have a class discussion about the brands and styles of athletic
   shoes teenagers are likely to buy.

   b) With a partner, choose one kind of shoe mentioned. Visit or
   phone a shoe store to find out the price of the shoe and its special
   features, what you do and/or do not find appealing about the
   shoe, and any promotional material on the shoe.

   c) Examine a magazine or TV advertisement for the shoe and note
   the information it contains and the product image it suggests.

   d) Present a brief report to the class explaining the similarities and
   differences between what you discovered about the shoe at the
   store and what the advertisement tells you.

3. With a partner, write a dialogue between a parent and a teenager
   about buying a pair of athletic shoes researched in 2(b) or something
   else the teenager really wants. Role play the dialogue for the class.

■ Personal and Imaginative Response

4. Develop a product for the teenage market. Draw or make a
   prototype of the product. Choose an image for your product and
   make this image central to a poster or commercial that you create.

5. Research the design of a familiar item such as a household gadget.
   Prepare a brief presentation that includes what you like and dislike
   about the design, and how you think it might be improved.

Art for a Brave New World

BY ROBERT K. J. KILLHEFFER

Barbara Nessim's studio is the very image of the Manhattan, New York, artist's flat. The area is filled with all the tools of the trade: brushes, sponges, jars of paint and ink, spattered worktables. But what sets her studio apart are the computers, which, with a corner all their own, form the true center of her work space. "I still work with other materials of course," says Nessim, a working artist for more than two decades, "but I spend most of my time with the computers."

Programmers have been toying with computer graphics for decades, but it is only relatively recently that nonspecialists have been attracted to computer art. Nessim herself was one of the pioneers, getting involved in the early Eighties, when computer graphics were just gaining limited artistic acceptance in some circles. Many people in the art world, as in society at large, remain skeptical of

computers, but Nessim hopes to introduce them to the possibilities with her "Random Access Memories" exhibition, which opened at New York's Rempire Fine Art and Gallery on April 11, 1991.

"Random Access Memories" consists of four displays: a series of three-dimensional "stereo pair" framed images, four poster-size single-image pastels, seven of Nessim's 6 x 9 foot [1.82 x 2.74 m] composite flags (each composed of 72 individual computer drawings), and a Macintosh-based interactive experience that yields each visitor a personalized miniature sketchbook. Although at first glance Nessim's work does not suggest the aid of computers, these displays would have been nearly impossible without them. The 3-D display, for instance, relies on two similar but slightly offset slide photographs—one for the left eye, one for the right—placed in a viewing device. The distinct images are

206

combined in the viewer's brain to create the illusion of depth.

The minute differences between the two slides would have been extremely difficult to manage by hand, but with the computer's help, Nessim could make the changes easily. Likewise, the interactive exhibit, which Nessim calls "the jewel of the show," couldn't exist apart from the computer. Nessim filled a database with more

than 200 drawings, and the gallery visitor uses the computer to select sketches to include in a miniature booklet, which the machine prints on the spot. "Everyone who comes will get a little gift," Nessim explains, "which not only serves as a souvenir from the show but is also a unique work of art. And they choose it themselves, they participate in it." Just as some writers are searching for ways to involve the reader more directly in the reading experience, Nessim has found a way to give the audience an active role in her display.

The computer offers artists a few clear advantages: minute control of the work, the power to make changes and corrections quickly and easily, and the ability to create multiple identical copies

of an item with minimal difficulty. But the computer has yet to produce a revolution in the art world. Most computer artists still rely on more traditional means for producing finished work: They use the computer to make rough sketches or, as in Nessim's case, components for a larger work developed outside the machine. High-quality plotters and printers are still prohibitively expensive, and even the best are limited in the sorts of effects they can create.

As long as such limitations exist, artistic applications of computer technology will be circumscribed as well. So for now the computer will remain an exotic design tool for interested artists, rather than an indispensable one for all. But as more galleries open

 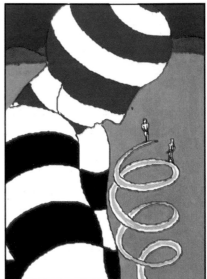

their doors to exhibitions of computer art, some sort of explosion cannot be far off. Some day Nessim predicts, the computer will become "like the telephone. You're not going to be able to live without one, and you're not going to want to." In that computerized world, work like hers will find a natural home.

Activities ART FOR A BRAVE NEW WORLD

■ Content and Style

1. a) As a class, make a list of the technical words in this article that are new to you. Using the resources available to you in class, define as many of these words as you can.

    b) Find other in-school resources (human or print) to help you with the remaining definitions.

    c) Create a computer graphics glossary and keep it for future reference.

2. With a partner, copy the chart below into your notebook. Write the main idea of the article in the box. Choose the major supporting ideas and write them in the other spaces.

Supporting Point #1   Supporting Point #2

_____   _____

_____   _____

> Main Idea
>
> _____
>
> _____

Supporting Point #3   Supporting Point #4

_____   _____

_____   _____

■ Social Context

3. a) Make a list of the ways computers are used in everyday life. Consider banking, shopping, entertainment, communication, the arts, and so on.

   b) Compare your list with a partner's. Add any ideas you may have missed.

   c) Choose one of the uses on your list. Write a speech proving that computers have had either a positive or a negative effect on our lives. Use examples to support your opinion. Present your speech to classmates.

■ Personal and Imaginative Response

4. a) Find out where computers are used in your school (e.g., office, guidance department).

   b) Choose a person from one of these areas and conduct an interview. Ask how computer technology is used and what it contributes to the school.

   c) Record and replay or write up the interview for classmates.

5. Imagine that you could go back in time and talk to someone from the beginning of the twentieth century. Write a dialogue explaining how computer technology affects one aspect of your life. Imagine how the person from the past might respond, and capture his or her feelings in your conversation.

6. Use a graphics program to create your own computer art. Display your work in the classroom along with a one-paragraph explanation of your reason for selecting the program you chose.

Dancers Are Athletes of the Arts World

BY KATHRYN GREENAWAY

What do you get when you combine physical prowess with artistic soul? Dancers. Call them the athletes of the arts world.

You've heard it all before. Up to six days a week, eight hours a day, they physically struggle for technical perfection. A dancer is never satisfied with the image in the mirror.

Think of it like you would a swimmer who battles daily to shave a full second off his or her best time.

Classical dancers begin their training early while the body is still malleable. But the career span is short. The average retirement age is 30.

At age 10 the sacrifices begin. You take ballet class instead of joining junior cheerleaders or the local ski club. Then dance mantras develop; *Don't stay out late. You'll be too tired to take class* and *Dance before anything else.*

A modern dancer's training begins later in life. Doing pointe work—which means dancing on your toes—is not part of the modern-dance curriculum, so the malleability of the feet and ankles is not as crucial.

Scene I: An electric guitar blasts high-voltage chords at two muscular performers as the woman pivots on her heel and snatches her male partner out of mid-air. She eases him to the ground and propels herself into a horizontal flip.

It's awesome to those who watch. It's physically excruciating to those who do.

Scene II: Enter lead La La La Human Steps dancer Louise Lecavalier. She is talking about her training program, eating habits and commitment to the profession, and as she gestures her biceps ripple.

Lecavalier began training as a modern dancer at age 18 and she's been carrying a heavy dance load with La La La since 1983.

The strength of female dancers has never been more challenged

211

since Montreal troupes like La La La developed unisex partnering in the early '80s. Now girls lift boys as much as boys lift girls.

Company class on tour consists of very fast, isolated, arm and torso movements; non-stop jumping to increase cardiovascular capacity; pushups; situps; leg exercises; and stretching.

Lecavalier increases the challenge by sewing tiny weights all over her practice outfit. Everything is geared to the high-impact cardiovascularity of the troupe's repertoire.

Prior to the show the dancers run around the stage to pump the heart rate up to a performance high.

In Montreal Lecavalier regularly takes ballet class and occasionally works out with free weights.

She's a self-confessed perfectionist, and even with the company on holiday for three months, she's at the studio six days a week working out. Eating also plays an important part in her training program.

"In the morning I eat things like oatmeal that will sustain me for many hours and I try to eat healthy things like fish or pasta when we're touring," Lecavalier said.

With so much physical stress to contend with injuries happen.

Lecavalier has torn the muscle in her calf twice in the last three years.

"For any person who works eight hours a day with their body, eventually something will happen. You have to learn to cope with it," Lecavalier said.

Commitment to the art crosses all style barriers. Exit the obvious athletics of La La La. Enter a subtler muscular control.

Scene III: The curtain rises and a tiny-framed ballet dancer floats across the stage on her toes.

Her leg effortlessly extends above her brow and her male partner plucks her up and over his head as if she were a mere apparition.

An example of the universal classical dancer's credo in action. *Make it look easy.*

Scene IV: Enter Anik Bissonnette and Louis Robitaille. The husband and wife team were the principal partnership with Ballet de Montreal Eddy Toussaint for 10 years, and now dance with Les Grands Ballets Canadiens.

The couple sticks closely to a rigid training routine. After nine hours of sleep, they begin their day with a protein mix called Budwig, whole wheat toast, and coffee.

By 9:30 AM they're in the studio dressed in tights and leg warmers and stretching out the aches and pains from the day before. This is followed by 90 minutes of non-stop exercise directed by a ballet teacher.

They work on the way the head, arms and legs can co-ordinate in different combinations: the height of the jump; the number of times they can turn on one leg (pirouettes); and the extension (how high you can lift your leg.)

The focus and discipline required is similar to that of a diver practising a triple twist. Where should my head be at what moment? When should my body straighten out?

"Almost all the girls at Les Grands take the class in pointe shoes," Bissonnette said in an interview.

It's common for women to lose their toenails because of pointe work, but due to the frequency of the occurrence it's not considered a serious affliction — just one more discomfort to contend with.

The men often augment their regular training with free-weight or Nautilus workouts to help them with lifts.

During ballet class, the teacher uses much the same tactics as an athletic coach would during a training session; humorous cajoling, verbal abuse and sarcastic remarks, plus the occasional pat on the back are common.

After class, comes five hours of rehearsal. Ballets for a coming performance are dissected and corrected, or a new ballet is created step by step.

Either process drains the body, and injuries are commonplace. Both Robitaille and Bissonnette have stopped dancing for up to three months because of injury.

Tendonitis in the feet and knees, torn or pulled ligaments, and broken bones and stress fractures are common injuries to dancers.

Royal Victoria Hospital orthopedic surgeon Dr. Bernard Costello has worked with dozens of injured dancers since 1981, and says that it's the repetition of movements that can be a dancer's nemesis.

"Dancers often repeat the same movement (in rehearsal) hundreds of times in one day. This puts incredible strain on whatever area of the body the move involves," Costello said in a recent interview.

"Dancers are the most motivated people I've ever seen as far as wanting to get back to work is concerned."

But this eagerness is not merely a display of dedication to the profession. "Dancers push to go back too soon because they're afraid to get out of shape. And sometimes, depending on the company, they're afraid to lose their jobs," Robitaille said.

The average dancer retires without any savings in the bank, no marketable skills and multiple memories of inflamed tendons, burning muscles and disintegrating toenails. So why bother? That's where the part about artistic soul comes in.

![Activities] **DANCERS ARE ATHLETES OF THE ARTS WORLD**

■ Content and Style

1. a) As you read through the article, write down any words you do not know the meaning of, as well as the sentence in which the word appears.

   b) With a partner, use the sentence to decide the meaning of each word.

   c) Review the words and the meanings you have listed. Look up the dictionary definition for each word to see how closely your definition matches it.

2. a) List the goals that dancers must work towards daily. Next to each goal, write "pc" (physical challenge), "mc" (mental challenge), or "pmc" (physical and mental challenge). Share your list with a partner.

   b) Make a list of goals you have for yourself, using the same abbreviations for the physical and mental challenges.

■ Social Context

3. Research information about a famous dancer of the past or present. Prepare a report on poster board that includes the following:
   • some pictures of the dancer performing (if available)
   • a summary of the dancer's personal background and history
   • a summary of the dancer's beliefs about dance
   • a summary of the dancer's contributions to dance and the personal challenges he or she faces
   • three quotations spoken by or about the dancer
   Display your finished report.

■ Personal and Imaginative Response

4. a) Select Scene I, II, III, or IV as described in the article and capture its mood in a poem of your own.

   b) Collect pictures from magazines that support the message of your poem. Use them to create a collage to go along with your poem.

   c) Display your poem and collage in the classroom.

5. Research an artistic, athletic, or recreational activity that interests you. Find out what kind of physical training is required to be successful in that activity. Share your findings with the class. Include a description of someone whom you regard as a role model in the activity you have studied.

All the Right Moves

BY BARRY CAME

André Simard's class begins promptly on weekday mornings at 9, as in any normal school. By almost every other measure, however, the instruction is extraordinary. The classroom is a huge cavern inside a converted railway station in downtown Montreal, and Simard's teaching method appears to consist largely of hauling furiously on ropes and pulleys while barking advice through his long, shaggy beard. His students are also unusual. They include youngsters like Xavier Lamoureux, a muscular 15-year-old with a dyed blond forelock who, on one recent morning, was hurtling through the air 32 feet [9.75 m] above the floor on a wildly rushing trapeze. By his side, Marie-Josée Lévesque, 21, swung slowly on a more sedate trapeze, balanced on her head. Below, 18-year-old Jennifer Tellier and Robert Bourgeois, 24, were fluidly entwined as they slid across a thin ribbon of steel. "They are all mad, of course," said Simard, a 47-year-old former Olympic high-bar gymnast, as the class drew to a close.

"But you have to be a little mad to want to study in this place."

Simard's version of a classroom is L'École Nationale de Cirque, the National Circus School. For the past 12 years, the singular Montreal institution has been capturing the imagination of young people seduced by the age-old desire to run away and join the circus. It has given hundreds of hopefuls an authentic taste of circus life and helped to transform the talented few into fully fledged—and gainfully employed—circus artists.

The National Circus School is, in many ways, unique. Unlike the majority of circus schools in the world, which are owned and operated by professional circus companies, the National is completely autonomous. There are no other institutions of the kind in North America offering both full-time training in the circus arts and a comprehensive high-school and junior-college academic program. Ten teachers and five administrators make up the staff.

The student body is divided into three categories. There are now 26 adults and six younger people, aged 9 to 16, enrolled in the full-time professional program. Another 15 students, mostly children, attend initiation classes three time a week. Finally, 125 youngsters and between 40 and 60 adults show up for weekly sessions specifically designed for people who, as Jan Rok Achard, the school's director, said, "want to learn a little about the circus just for the sheer fun of it all."

It is the professional program, however, that is the National School's main focus. Each of the 32 students now in the program appears to have been terminally afflicted by circus madness. Each pays $1600 annually to participate in 35 to 40 weeks of gruelling, individually tailored instruction aimed at turning out an accomplished circus performer eventually capable of gaining employment in a professional circus company. Those determined young hopefuls can be found in the morning working on fundamentals in the school's gymnasium, on makeup and costumes in the wardrobe room, studying in the basement or developing routines in the enormous 71 1/2-foot-high [22-m-high] classroom they call the *chapiteau*—the big top.

Jennifer Tellier hauled herself from the gymnasium's "crash pit," filled with 12 150 yellow foam cubes, to explain the reasons that persuade a freckle-faced 18-year-old to submit to the daily punishing grind. "Sure it's tough sometimes," said the Montreal native, a student at the school for the past two years, "but I've always been a kind of hyperactive kid. And from the moment I saw my first circus, I just knew deep down that it was a world that I badly wanted to belong to."

Many students have been drawn by the National's growing international renown. For the past four years, all of the National's entrants in competition at the Paris-based Festival of the Circus of Tomorrow, an annual event open to both professionals and circus students under 25, have won medals. That kind of success on the world stage has resulted in invitations for the school to participate in performances in locations as diverse as Verona, Italy, and Wuhan, China. It is also reflected in the fact that seven of the 32 students enrolled in the current professional program are from outside Canada—four from France, two from the United States and one from Switzerland. There are likely to be more in the future: of the 83 applications that the school has received for the 12 places available in the professional program next year, no fewer than 81 are from foreigners.

Shana Carroll, 21, of San Francisco, hopes to be one of the

lucky dozen. She is currently enrolled in a basic introductory program at the National. She had been performing as a trapeze artist at San Francisco's Pickle Family Circus, a small, politically oriented troupe, but decided that she needed advanced instruction. She said that she went to Montreal for two reasons. "The National is the only school in North America, and maybe one of the few schools anywhere else in the world, that still focuses on the circus as an art form rather than all the tired old stuff you get in places like Ringling and Barnum and Bailey," said Carroll, taking a break from a choreography lesson on the floor of the *chapiteau*. The other motivating factor was teacher André Simard. "He's the best," she said. "In terms of trapeze, there's simply no one better."

Simard dismisses praise with a shrug, but in fact, he is one of the National's prime assets. After competing, unsuccessfully, in the 1972 Munich Olympics, he went on to coach the Canadian national

gymnastic team for seven years before joining the staff of the Montreal school in 1988. While fond of describing himself as "nothing but a technician," he is responsible for helping to implement one of the school's abiding principles. "I'm basically a guide rather than a teacher," he said. "I try to help each of these kids see where their particular strengths and weaknesses lie so they can go on to develop their own distinctive style and technique." He added: "If they get it right, if they can make the impossible look easy, then it's nothing short of magic." Magic, and maybe just a little mad, too.

Activities   ALL THE RIGHT MOVES

■ Content and Style

1. List three things students of the National Circus School have done that suggest it is a successful school. Compare your list with that of a classmate.

2. In one paragraph for each, identify and explain three ways in which the National Circus School is different from a typical high school. In another paragraph, explain whether you would rather attend your school or the National.

3. a) In a group, brainstorm five questions about the National Circus School or circus life that are not answered in the article.

   b) Research the information to answer your questions.

■ Social Context

4. The circus school has both adults and young people working and studying together. With a partner, prepare a brief presentation to the class. Explain whether or not you think adults and teens should attend the same schools.

5. Students at the National Circus School pay tuition. With a partner, prepare a brief presentation for the class explaining why student tuition is or is not a good idea.

6. With a partner, prepare a brief presentation to the class on whether you think high schools should focus more on job skills or on general knowledge.

■ Personal and Imaginative Response

7. With the help of the library or your school guidance department, make a list of other specialized schools in Canada and their area of specialization. Prepare a poster advertising one or more of these schools to hang in your guidance office.

8. Write and perform a radio advertisement for the National Circus School that would inform students in your school and might encourage them to apply.

9. Create a brochure for a specialized high school that you might like to attend, such as a High School of International Business, a High School of Ballet, or a Basketball Collegiate.

10. Using information from "All the Right Moves," write a diary entry that describes a day in the life of one of the students.

Captain Canuck

BY RICHARD COMELY

D arren Oak is Captain Canuck. Born and raised in a wealthy and powerful family, he becomes a champion kick boxer and sets up a centre for homeless people. Darren discovers that his older brother Nathan, who controls the family empire, is involved in a conspiracy to destroy Canada. In desperation, Darren puts on a costume inspired by a comic book character and sets out to warn the Canadian public of his brother's evil plan.

Creators of Captain Canuck

Captain Canuck was "born" in 1971 when Ron Leishman presented the idea of a Canadian super hero to artist Richard Comely. Comely wrote and published the first issue of the comic book in 1975, as well as 14 issues between then and 1981. Although Comely had some financial problems that caused him to take a break, Captain Canuck returned in 1993 with new storylines and an updated image. Richard Comely continues to be involved in all aspects of the comic, including the writing, artwork, and distribution.

■ Content and Style

1. With a partner, list five or more characteristics of super heroes. Decide how Captain Canuck fits into the mold of the typical super hero.

2. The creator of this excerpt from a Captain Canuck comic book uses the background of characters in a film shoot stepping out of their role to insult each other. In groups, decide why the creator did this.

3. Comics use the techniques of film such as close-ups, medium shots and long shots, and low and high angles. Cut a comic strip out of the newspaper and label each frame as if it were drawn on a storyboard.

■ Social Context

4. Some Canadian critics point out that most of the popular culture we consume is American and that Canadians should encourage the creation of our own "popular culture." As a class, decide whether you think Captain Canuck is helping to create our own popular culture.

5. With a partner, determine to what extent Captain Canuck is a comic that reflects the desires, fears, and hopes of our society. Report your conclusions to the class.

■ Personal and Imaginative Response

6. In groups, design your own cover for a new issue of Captain Canuck. Use information you have learned about the creator and his characters. Show it to the rest of the class and ask them to
   • guess the plot, and
   • decide how true your cover is to the spirit of Captain Canuck.

7. With a partner, outline a plot that could grow out of these characters and their plans for the world.

8. Debate the following resolution: Comic books are dangerous because they offer us unrealistic ways to escape from the difficult problems of the world.

Toronto's Homeless Turn to the Bard

BY CLYDE H. FARNSWORTH

Toronto—The more printable graffiti on the hulking bridge columns over the rail yards and abandoned warehouses at Bathurst Street read, "Welcome to Hotel Hell" and "Eat the Rich."

Until they were chased out by fire hoses a few months ago, hundreds of street youths and other homeless people lived in this industrial underbelly several hundred metres from polluted waters of Lake Ontario, within the shadows of the CN Tower and the Skydome.

Now, thanks to an extraordinary production of *Romeo and Juliet*, sponsored by an organization that uses theater as a vehicle for teaching job skills, communication and self-esteem to street youths, some of the homeless have returned as performers and technicians.

Shakespeare in the wasteland with its bubbling energy and imagination—a set pieced together of pipes, axles, tires, hubcaps, and other junk from the site; garlands from Queen Anne's lace and yellow yarrow growing here—has become both a forum for the youths and a source of money for helping them.

"There are thousands and thousands of desperate youth who have no prospects for a better future," said Ned Dickens, the show's producer. "We're trying to show that you really can do something for them that means something."

Official city figures count 30 000 homeless people in Toronto, Canada's biggest and richest city. About half are under 18.

Dickens is director of the Kensington Youth Theatre and Employment Skills, a local organization known as KYTES, that helps street youths change their way of life through the staging of theatrical works for the public.

Troupe members not only create theater, but also upgrade themselves academically, find stable housing and confront alcohol or drug use and other problems arising from anger at parents and

226

society. Every year, more than 200 youths apply for 44 places. Each member gets high school credit during the five-month program.

Romeo and Juliet is more ambitious than most Kensington productions. Several professionals, including young actors in and out of theater school, donate their talents. Kensington lost a federal grant this year and is using the show to help raise money.

"Romeo and Juliet are real accessible characters for young people," said Sarah Stanley, 30, one of the professionals who directs the play. She has also worked in Paris and Montreal.

"They are teenagers who follow their desires to the end of their lives. Juliet is threatened by her father. Both she and Romeo decide to defy what's expected of them. There is a real analogy to be drawn."

Katrin Clouse, 20, calls herself a "positive statistic." Four years ago, after her mother remarried,

she had left home, dropped out of high school, and was out on bail after being charged with car theft.

"Things were pretty troubled in my life," she recalled after a stunning performance as Juliet. "I just didn't think about the future."

She had been living as a vagrant on Yonge Street in Toronto when she was accepted into the Kensington program. "Now I'm doing a payback of sorts." Next month, she enters the University of Toronto, where she is thinking of studying law or journalism.

Mastering the lines, she said, was like "learning Japanese." Then during rehearsals a few weeks ago, "the part suddenly spoke out."

Clouse said she identified with the adolescent Juliet's feelings of frustration and entrapment in the feud of the older generation. She also found "on the mark" Shakespeare's depiction of the lack of communication between the two generations.

She didn't much like Shakespeare's ending, however. "I would never kill myself, especially not for a guy."

Jason Cadieux, 18, a sensitive, ardent, vigorous Romeo, attends an alternative high school in Toronto, plays bass guitar in his own band, and wants to make acting his career, "feast or famine."

Another "positive statistic" is Irwin Quigley, 24, the lightboard-operator. On the streets since he was 14, he learned his electrician's skills at Kensington and expects to parlay these into permanent work. He is also head of security for the troupe of 100 people, who have made both a stage and sleeping quarters of the old illegal dump site beneath the bridge.

A tent stands behind the makeshift stage and serves as the dressing room. It is also the sleeping quarters for about 10 members of the troupe who stand watch over the equipment in shifts. Some have nowhere else to go.

Canadian National Railways owns the land and gave Kensington permission to use it. Now every night hundreds of people walk down a weedy dirt path into this theater where monarch butterflies hover over milkweed and purple thistle and actors battle, dance or roll in the dirt.

Viewers sit on plastic milk cartons listening to a production that must compete with sirens, helicopters, trains, and, every few minutes, another streetcar rumbling overhead on Bathurst Street.

Capulet, played by Jim Donnelly, gets an unscripted laugh when, affrighted, he asks: "What noise is this? Give me my long sword ho!"

But audiences love it, and so do the reviewers. "What you actually see," wrote H. J. Kirchhoff, theater critic for *The Globe and Mail,* "is decent Shakespeare."

■ Content and Style

1. Based on the information in the article, list the following:
   - the skills the teenagers learned
   - how they learned these skills

   With a partner, brainstorm other ways teens could learn the skills you listed.

2. Write in your notebook descriptive details that help create the urban setting of this article. Make a list of descriptive words and phrases that you would use to create a sense of place when writing an article about an event in your community.

■ Social Context

3. Invite a youth worker to your class to speak about the challenges facing street youth. As a class, prepare questions before the worker visits.

4. Write to one of the organizations that provides services for street youth. Ask them to send you information about their service.

5. In a small group, prepare a presentation you could make to a minister of the federal or provincial government explaining why KYTES should or should not receive funding. Perform your presentation for classmates.

■ Personal and Imaginative Response

6. In a group of three, find two or three short dramatic pieces that present issues about young people. The librarian or a drama teacher will be able to help you.
   a) Compile a class list of the selections you found.
   b) Choose one selection for performance and prepare to present it to an audience.

To Amy Lowell

BY WINFIELD TOWNLEY SCOTT

I can remember now
How I felt
When I first read your words.
It was like finding
Purple and white crocuses
Poking thru brown leaves of autumn
That had lingered on till spring.
Your words flash fire,
Gyrating red, blue, yellow, orange rings
And rockets flaming upward.
Then again
You are cold,
Talking of graves and such.
But I love you most
When you send cool words
Rippling along as a brook
Plays over stones at dawn,
Or as a shepherd boy,
Lying alone upon a meadow green,
Pipes softly on an instrument of reeds.
And then the other morning
I picked up the paper
And read the queerest news.
AMY LOWELL DIES, the headlines screamed.
Well, I was rather taken aback,
You may believe.
But I had an idea the paper was in error—
You know how they do confuse things.
So I raced upstairs to the bookshelf,
Opened one of your little volumes and found

That I was right—
The paper was in error.
For there you were,
Just as you always had been—
The rockets and the pinwheels and the cold.
And best of all—
There were the soft words
That look so pretty running on the page—
Little letters on the white paper you talk so much about.
It was as if a fresh breeze,
Blowing across the hot room,
Had cooled my cheek.
I felt as though I had dipped my hand
Into a garden pool at night
Where were reflected heaven and the stars;
And while the cold water swam about my wrist,
I held the stars
And let them run
Between my fingers!

■ Content and Style

1. a) Choose three images or word pictures the poet has created. Write them down in your notebook.

    b) With a partner, compare the images you have chosen. Discuss how the poet uses words to help you form clear pictures in your imagination.

2. a) In a short paragraph, state the subject and theme of the poem. Refer to the poem to explain how you arrived at your decision.

    b) In a group of three, discuss each of your paragraphs. Agree on the main subject and theme of the poem.

■ Social Context

3. As a class, decide when you think this poem was written. Use clues from the poem to support your opinion.

4. List five poems and/or songs that have had a strong effect on you. Explain why they affected you so much.

■ Personal and Imaginative Response

5. In a group of three, prepare this poem for presentation. Decide what is the best way to use three voices. Choose a piece of music as background to your reading.

6. Through a series of drawings, re-create two of the pictures that the poet tried to capture in words. Consider not only the images but also the mood that the author created.

7. With another student, find two poems written by Amy Lowell as well as some information about her. Prepare a bulletin board display that combines the poetry and information you have found with photographs or artwork.

Johnnie's Poem

BY ALDEN NOWLAN

Look! I've written a poem!
Johnnie says
and hands it to me
     and it's about
     his grandfather dying
     last summer, and me
     in the hospital
and I want to cry,
don't you see, because it doesn't matter
if it's not very good:
     what matters is he knows
and it was me, his father, who told him
     you write poems about what
     you feel deepest and hardest.

■ Content and Style

1. a) Decide which one or two lines in this poem are the most powerful or meaningful. Write them in your notebook.

   b) Write one or two paragraphs explaining what appealed to you about the lines you chose.

2. In a group, brainstorm ideas about what makes a poem good or bad. Write one or two guidelines for judging the quality of a work of art. Share your guidelines with the class.

■ Social Context

3. Think about a family member or other person who has touched your life. Write a letter to that person explaining what she or he means to you.

■ Personal and Imaginative Response

4. Write a poem that expresses strong feelings you have about someone or something. You might use "Johnnie's Poem" as a model.

5. In a group of three, write a script in which a grandfather, father, and son share an important experience together. (Feel free to substitute female roles, e.g., grandmother, mother, and daughter.) Perform or videotape the scene.

The Author

BY M. E. KERR

Before the author comes to school, we all have to write him, saying we are glad he is coming and we like his books.

That is Ms. Terripelli's idea. She is our English teacher and she was the one who first got the idea to have real, live authors visit Leighton Middle School.

She wants the author to feel welcome.

You are my favorite author, I write.

I have never read anything he's written.

Please send me an autographed picture, I write. I am sure this will raise my English grade, something I need desperately, since it is not one of my best subjects.

The truth is: I have best friends and best clothes and best times, but not best subjects.

I am going to be an author, too, someday, I write, surprised to see the words pop up on the screen. But I am writing on the computer in the school library and there is something wonderful about the way any old thought can become little green letters in seconds, which you can erase with one touch of your finger.

I don't push WordEraser, however.

I like writing that I am going to become an author.

The person I am writing to is Peter Sand.

My name happens to be Peter too.

Peter Sangetti.

I might shorten my name to Peter Sang, when I become an author, I write. *Then maybe people will buy my books by mistake, thinking they are getting yours. (Ha! Ha!)*

Well, I write, *before this turns into a book and you sell it for money, I will sign off, but I will be looking for you when you show up at our school.*

I sign it *Sincerely*, although that's not exactly true.

The night before the author visit, my dad comes over to see me. My stepfather and my mother have gone off to see my stepbrother, Tom, in Leighton High School's version of *The Sound of Music.*

To myself, and sometimes to my mother, I call him Tom Terrific. Naturally, he has the lead in the musical. He is Captain Von Trapp. If they ever make the Bible into a play, he will be God.

I like him all right, but I am tired of playing second fiddle to him always. He is older, smarter, and better looking, and his last name is Prince. Really.

I can't compete with him.

It's funny, because the first words out of my dad's mouth that night are, "I can't compete with that."

He is admiring the new CD audio system my stepfather had ordered from the Sharper Image catalog. It is an Aiwa with built-in BBE sound.

"It's really for Tom Terrific," I say, but it is in the living room, not Tom's bedroom, and Dad knows my CD collection is my pride and joy.

I suppose just as I try to compete with Tom Terrific, my dad tries to compete with Thomas Prince, Sr.... Both of us are losing the game, it seems. My dad is even out of work now, although it is our secret...not to be shared with my mom or stepfather.

The plant where he worked was closed. He'd have to move out of the state to find the same kind of job he had there, and he doesn't want to leave me.

"I'm not worried about you," I lie. And then I hurry to change the subject, and tell him about the author's visit, next day.

He smiles and shakes his head. "Funny. I once wanted to be a writer."

"I never knew that."

"Sure. One time I got this idea for a story about our cat. She was always sitting in the window of our apartment building, looking out. She could never get out, but she'd sit there, and I'd think it'd be her dream come true if she could see a little of the world! Know what I mean, Pete?"

"Sure I do." I also know that my dad always wished he could travel. He is the only person I've ever known who actually reads *National Geographic.*

He laughs. "So I invented a story about the day she got out. Here was her big chance to run around the block!"

"What happened?"

"A paper bag fell from one of the apartments above ours. It landed right on Petunia's head. She ran around the block, all right, but she didn't see a thing."

Both of us roar at the idea, but deep down I don't think it is that hilarious, considering it is my dad who dreamed it up.

What's he think—that he'll never see the world? Never have his dreams come true?

"Hey, what's the matter?" he says. "You look down in the dumps suddenly."

"Not me," I say.

"Aw, that was a dumb story," he says. "Stupid!"

"It was fine," I say.

"No, it wasn't," he says. "I come over here and say things to spoil your evening. You'd rather hear your music."

"No, I wouldn't," I say, but he is getting up to go.

We are losing touch not living in the same house anymore.

Whenever I go over to his apartment, he spends a lot of time apologizing for it. It is too small. It isn't very cheerful. It needs a woman's touch. I want to tell him that if he'd just stop pointing out all the things wrong with it, I'd like it fine…but it is turning out that we aren't great talkers anymore. I don't say everything on my mind anymore.

He shoots me a mock punch at the door and tells me that next week he'll get some tickets to a hockey game. Okay with me? I say he doesn't have to, thinking of the money, and he says I know it's not like going to the World Series or anything. I'd gone to the World Series the year before with my stepfather.

"Let up," I mumble.

"What?" he says.

"Nothing."

He says, "I heard you, Pete. You're right. You're right."

Next day, waiting for me out front is Ms. Terripelli.

"He asked for you, Pete! You're going to be Mr. Sand's guide for the day."

"Why me?" I ask.

"Because you want to be a writer?" She looks at me and I look at her.

"Oh, that," I say.

"You never told the class that," she says.

"It's too personal."

"Do you write in secret, Pete?"

"I have a lot of ideas," I say.

"Good for you!" says Ms. Terripelli, and she hands me a photograph of Peter Sand. It is autographed. It also has written on it, "Maybe someday I'll be asking for yours, so don't change your name. Make me wish it was mine, instead."

"What does all this mean?" Ms. Terripelli asks me.

"Just author stuff," I say.

I put the picture in my locker and go to the faculty lounge to meet him.

He is short and plump, with a moustache. He looks like a little colonel of some sort, because he has this booming voice and a way about him that makes you feel he knows his stuff.

"I never write fantasy," he says. "I write close to home. When you read my books, you are reading about something that happened to me!… Some authors write both fantasy and reality!"

238

At the end of his talk he answers all these questions about his books and he autographs paperback copies.

I hang out with him the whole time.

We don't get to say much to each other until lunch.

The school doesn't dare serve him what we get in the cafeteria, so they send out for heroes, and set up a little party for him in the lounge.

The principal shows up, and some librarians from the Leighton Town Library.

When we do get a few minutes to talk, he asks me what I am writing.

I say, "We had this cat, Petunia, who was always looking out the window…"

He is looking right into my eyes as though he is fascinated, and I finish the story.

"Wow!" he says. "Wow!"

"It's sort of sad," I say.

"It has heart and it has humor, Pete," he says. "The best stories always do."

His last session is in the school library, and members of the town are invited.

About fifty people show up.

He talks about his books for a while, and then he starts talking about me.

He tells the story of Petunia. He called it wistful and amusing, and he says anyone who can think up a story like that knows a lot about the world already.

I get a lot of pats on the back afterward, and Ms. Terripelli says, "Well, you've had quite a day for yourself, Pete."

By this time I am having trouble looking her in the eye.

Things are a little out of hand, but what the heck—he is on his way to the airport and back to Maine, where he lives. What did it hurt that I told a few fibs?

Next day, the *Leighton Lamplighter* has the whole story. I hadn't even known there was a reporter present. There is the same photograph Peter Sand has given to me, and there is my name in the article about the author visit.

My name. Dad's story of Petunia, with no mention of Dad.

"Neat story!" says Tom Terrific.

My stepfather says if I show him a short story all finished and ready to send out somewhere, he'll think about getting me a word processor.

239

"I don't write for gain," I say.

Mom giggles. "You're a wiseguy, Pete."

"Among other things," I say.

Like a liar, I am thinking. Like a liar and a cheat.

When Dad calls, I am waiting for the tirade.

He has a bad temper. He is the type who leaves nothing unsaid when he blows. I expect him to blow blue: he does when he loses his temper. He comes up with slang that would knock the socks off the Marine Corps.

"Hey, Pete," he says, "you really liked my story, didn't you?"

"Too much, I guess. That's why you didn't get any credit."

"What's mine is yours, kid. I've always told you that."

"I went off the deep end, I guess, telling him I want to be a writer."

"An apple never falls far from the tree, Pete. That was my ambition when I was your age."

"Yeah, you told me…. But *me*. What do I know?"

"You have a good imagination, son. And you convinced Peter Sand what you were saying was true."

"I'm a good liar, I guess."

"Or a good storyteller…. Which one?"

Why does he have to say which one?

Why does he have to act so pleased to have given me something?

The story of Petunia isn't really a gift. I realize that now. It was more like a loan.

I can tell the story, just as my dad told it to me, but when I try to turn myself from a liar into a storyteller, it doesn't work on paper.

I fool around with it for a while. I try.

The thing is: fantasy is not for me.

I finally find out what it is when I come up with a first sentence which begins:

Before the author comes to school, we all have to write him, saying we are glad he is coming and we like his books.

You see, I'm an author who writes close to home.

Activities THE AUTHOR

■ Content and Style

1. Select four details of family and/or school life the author has included that give the story a ring of truth. Explain to a partner the choices you make.

2. Write a brief explanation of why the father's story of the cat upsets Peter.

3. As Peter, write a brief statement about what you hope young people will learn from reading this story.

■ Social Context

4. Many young people have both parents and step-parents. Write two reasons why you feel this story does or does not describe how young people with more than two parents feel.

5. With a partner, suggest two examples for each of the following:
   • situations in which it is never right to lie
   • situations in which it is not wrong to lie
   • situations in which it may even be helpful to lie
   Present your examples to classmates.

■ Personal and Imaginative Response

6. Write a story about a lie someone told and what happened afterwards.

7. Explain in writing why you prefer to read fiction or non-fiction.

8. a) Write a letter to Peter advising him about whether or not he should become a writer. Give reasons for your advice.
   b) Imagine that Peter sends his second story ("The Author") to Peter Sand. Write a letter that the older author might prepare in response.

9. What would have happened if Peter's father had been angry about Peter's use of his story? Write and perform the dialogue Peter and his father might have had the day after the newspaper story appeared.

Living Twice

BY NATALIE GOLDBERG

Writers live twice. They go along with their regular life, are as fast as anyone in the grocery store, crossing the street, getting dressed for work in the morning. But there's another part of them that they have been training. The one that lives everything a second time. That sits down and sees their life again and goes over it. Looks at the texture and details.

In a rainstorm, everyone quickly runs down the street with umbrellas, raincoats, newspapers over their heads. Writers go back outside in the rain with a notebook in front of them and a pen in hand. They look at the puddles, watch them fill, watch the rain splash in them. You can say a writer practices being dumb. Only a dummy would stand out in the rain and watch a puddle. If you're smart, you get in out of the rain so you won't catch cold, and you have health insurance, in case you get sick. If you're dumb, you are more interested in the puddle than in your security and insurance or in getting to work on time.

You're more interested, finally, in living life again in your writing than in making money. Now, let's understand—writers do like money; artists, contrary to popular belief, do like to eat. It's only that money isn't the driving force. I feel very rich when I have time to write and very poor when I get a regular paycheck and no time to work at my real work. Think of it. Employers pay salaries for time. That is the basic commodity that human beings have that is valuable. We exchange our time in life for money. Writers stay with the first step—their time—and feel it is valuable even before they get money for it. They hold on to it and aren't so eager to sell it. It's like inheriting land from your family. It's always been in your family: they have always owned it. Someone comes along and wants to buy it. Writers, if they are

242

smart, won't sell too much of it. They know once it's sold, they might be able to buy a second car, but there will be no place they can go to sit still, no place to dream on.

So it is good to be a little dumb when you want to write. You carry that slow person inside you who needs time; it keeps you from selling it all away. That person will need a place to go and will demand to stare into rain puddles in the rain, usually with no hat on, and to feel the drops on her scalp.

Activities   LIVING TWICE

■ Content and Style

1. Divide your notebook into three columns. In the first column, record words or phrases from the selection that interested you. In the second column, record your response to the word or phrase. In the third column, have a classmate respond to the entries you made.

2. Use "Living Twice" as a model for writing about a hobby or activity you enjoy. Share your writing in a small group.

■ Social Context

3. a) In your own words write an explanation of the behaviour or lifestyle described by the author in this piece.

   b) Write her a letter expressing your thoughts on living life this way.

4. a) In a group, brainstorm some of the different jobs a professional writer might work at such as novel writing or journalism. Create a master list of writing careers to post in the classroom.

   b) Choose one career from the list and prepare a job profile. Your description might include information about the following:
   • needed education and skills
   • working environments and conditions
   • a day in the life of someone who does that kind of writing
   • the name of a writer who does that kind of writing
   Present your description to the class. Include a sample of writing developed by a writer you researched.

5. Explain in writing why writers are or are not needed in today's world.

■ Personal and Imaginative Response

6. Carefully look at something you usually don't take the time to notice. Look for the hidden beauty, detail, strangeness, or humour in what you are observing. Take detailed notes. Write a paragraph about your observations.

7. a) Watch a stranger waiting for a bus or subway or someone walking. Study the person's posture, walk, and clothing. Consider what his or her lifestyle and job might be. Imagine where the person might live.

   b) Practise being this person as you imitate things you noticed about his or her posture and movements. Observe yourself in the mirror to improve your characterization.

   c) Dramatize for a group how your person might behave in a specific situation. Do not use words. Ask the group to guess the kind of person you are characterizing.

1. Create a collage of words and images from magazines and newspapers that expresses your views about how technology affects you or society in general.

2. Choose a career in the arts or technology. Prepare a report that includes the following information:
   - what education you need
   - where you can get the education
   - salary range
   - working conditions

   Post your report on the class bulletin board.

3. Watch a television program about some aspect of the arts or technology. Prepare a report for the class in which you summarize the program and give your own evaluation of it.

4. One of the main themes in this unit is the lack of power we have in controlling technology. Using some of the selections as reference, have a class debate on the following resolution: Today technology is more our master than our servant.

5. Write a guide for parents on how to supervise their children's television viewing. Consider what age group would have parental supervision, the number of viewing hours, and how you believe parents could get involved in their children's viewing.

6. In his article "TV: Is It a One-Eyed Monster?" the author writes: "There have been complaints that many Saturday morning cartoons are nothing but half-hour commercials for toys!" Contact the Canadian Association of Broadcasters to request "The Broadcast Code for Advertising to Children" or locate a copy of it in the library. Read the report and decide whether the guidelines are adequate and, based on your own television viewing, whether they are being followed. Put your findings together in a report to the Canadian Association of Broadcasters in which you explain your concerns.

7. In the poem "Misery," Andrew Parker writes, "You want to leap through the TV into their world, /To put your hand out, to give their lives some stability." As a class, find a charity or cause you would like to support. For example, you may want to contact a church or community organization that is involved in a cause locally or in some other part of the world. When you have identified the charity or cause, do the following:

   • Set goals to determine what you will do.

   • Divide up responsibilities.

   • Write messages that you can deliver over the PA system to encourage the rest of the school to take part.

   • Organize collection times for any items you are giving to the charity or cause.

   When you have accomplished your goals, write a letter to the community paper to tell them about your project.

8. In the final section of this unit, The Arts in Action, people discuss different artistic activities, including poetry, dance, the circus, comic books, theatre, and writing. After reading these selections, decide which artistic activities seem to be missing from this section. Find two selections that focus on some of these missing activities. Then write a paragraph about each to convince the editor that these selections should be included in a revised version of the book.

Alternate Groupings of the Selections

Alienation
I Loved My Friend
Dying for Love
Meg's First Day
On the Bridge
Shinny Game Melted the Ice
I Lost My Talk
I Am Yours
Being Comfortable With Being "Weird"
Can't You See?
Ready, Willing and Able
No Place for Teenagers
The Essential Mallmanac
Interview With Victor Malarek
On the Sidewalk, Bleeding
Those Who Don't
A Tanned Version
On a Very Gray Day
Fear of the Landscape
The Iguana
A Warm Safe Bed
User Friendly
I Love You—This Is a Recording
Misery
Toronto's Homeless Turn to the Bard
The Author

Canadian Authors
Maria Bohuslawsky (No Place for Teenagers)
Martha Brooks (Dying for Love)
Barry Came (All the Right Moves)
Richard Comely (Captain Canuck)
Afua Cooper (My Mother)
Barry Duncan (TV: Is It a One-Eyed Monster?)
Mariam Khan Durrani (Can't You See?)

Kathryn Greenaway (Dancers Are Athletes of the Arts World)
Andrea Holtslander (Dave's Fall)
Monica Hughes (A Warm Safe Bed)
Rita Joe (I Lost My Talk)
Frank Jones ("Regular Guy" Becomes a Champion)
Keith Leckie (Words on a Page)
Janesse Leung (On a Very Gray Day)
Jean McCallion (Tough Roots)
Daniel Moses (Words on a Page)
Andrea Mozarowski (Interview With Victor Malarek, Interview
    With Peter Dalglish)
Alden Nowlan (Johnnie's Poem)
Andrew Parker (Misery)
Naomi C. Powell (Being Comfortable With Being "Weird")
Randy Starkman (Ready, Willing and Able)
David Suzuki (Living With Nature)
Judith Thompson (I Am Yours)
Richard Wagamese (Shinny Game Melted the Ice)
Ian Young (Fear of the Landscape)

Celebration of Life
Oranges
Dave's Fall
Dying for Love
Meg's First Day
Shinny Game Melted the Ice
My Mother
Words on a Page
Being Comfortable With Being "Weird"
Ready, Willing and Able
Take Time for 8 Matters of the Heart
Interview With Victor Malarek
Interview With Peter Dalglish
Capturing the Majesty of Nature
As I Walk Along the Hillside
Tough Roots
Stopping by Woods on a Snowy Evening
"Regular Guy" Becomes a Champion
December 2001: The Green Morning
A Warm Safe Bed

Humour

Author Biographies

T. Ernesto Bethancourt is of Puerto Rican descent and was born Thomas E. Passailaigue in 1932 in Brooklyn, New York. After dropping out of college, he worked as a singer, guitarist, and song-writer under the name of Tom Paisley. Later he became contributing editor for *High Fidelity* magazine. He first wrote books for young adults when he started writing an autobiography so that his daughter would know about his life: *New York City Too Far From Tampa Blues.* Since then, he has published a number of short novels, including *Where the Deer and the Cantaloupe Play* and *Tune in Yesterday.* "User Friendly" is the last thing he wrote with his old computer before it stopped working and had to be replaced. He lives in Brooklyn.

Maria Bohuslawsky has worked as a journalist for several years, first with *The Toronto Sun*, later the *Winnipeg Free Press*, and now *The Ottawa Citizen.* She has published one book called *End of the Line*, an inside story of life in Canadian nursing homes.

Ray Bradbury was born in 1920 in Waukegan, Illinois, and worked briefly as a newsboy in Los Angeles before becoming a full-time writer in 1942. Since that time he has written countless books, including short story collections, novels, plays, poetry anthologies, and movies. He is best known for his eerie science fiction stories and novels. He says he feels he should be thankful for his childhood fear of the dark because "You have to know fear and apprehension in some form before you can write about it thoroughly."

Martha Brooks was born in Ninette, Manitoba, in 1944 and grew up on the grounds of a tuberculosis hospital where her parents worked. She feels this isolation provided her with a distinct view of the world. She spent ten years writing before anyone would publish her work. Since then she has published a variety of novels, plays, and short stories. "Dying for Love" is taken from her collection *Paradise Cafe and Other Stories.* Brooks describes writing a story as "going across the Grand Canyon on a tightrope at midnight with no safety net."

Helen Caldicott, an Australian-born doctor who now lives in the United States, is an opponent of nuclear weapons and the arms race. She is the founder of Physicians for Social Responsibility and Women's Action for Nuclear Disarmament. She has published two books, *Nuclear Madness* and *Missile Envy*, and appeared in the National Film Board's award-winning film, *If You Love This Planet*.

Barry Came was born in 1943 in London, England, and educated at Carleton University in Ottawa. After starting his journalism career with the *Winnipeg Free Press*, he moved on to *The Globe and Mail* newspaper and *Newsweek* magazine. He now lives in Montreal, Quebec, and writes for *Maclean's* magazine.

Tyrone Cashman is president of the Solar Economy Institute in Mill Valley, California, and trained in the philosophy of biology. "Capturing the Majesty of Nature" appeared in the magazine *Media & Values*.

Sandra Cisneros was born in Chicago, Illinois, in 1954 to a Mexican father and American mother. She grew up in a Puerto Rican neighbourhood that served as the inspiration for *The House on Mango Street* from which "Those Who Don't" is taken. While attending Loyola University, she was introduced to Chicano writers for the first time and slowly came to recognize herself as one. She went on to the University of Iowa's Writers Workshop where she earned a Master of Fine Arts degree in 1978. She has published two collections of poetry. Her most recent book is *Woman Hollering Creek and Other Stories*.

Afua Cooper was born in Westmoreland, Jamaica, and grew up in Kingston, Jamaica. She moved to Toronto, Ontario, in 1980. She is the author of *Breaking Chains* and *The Red Caterpillar on College Street*. Her latest collection of poetry, *Memories Have Tongue*, from which "My Mother" is taken, explores both personal and public history.

Isak Dinesen is one of the pen names of Karen Blixen, who was born in Rungsted, Denmark, in 1885 and died there in 1962. She was taught at home by a governess and later attended the Royal

Academy of Fine Art in Copenhagen. She dropped out of the Academy and turned her hand to writing. At the encouragement of a friend she had her first story, "The Hermits," published in 1907 under the pen name Osceola. She married Baron Blixen and moved to British East Africa (now Kenya) where they managed a coffee plantation. She published several books about her life in Africa, including her most famous, *Out of Africa*, which was made into a movie in 1984.

Barry Duncan attended the University of Western Ontario and the University of Toronto, where he studied under communications scholar, Marshall McLuhan. He is the founder and president of the Association for Media Literacy and wrote the textbook *Mass Media and Popular Culture*. He has taught at the University of Toronto and the Harvard Graduate School of Education, and made presentations to thousands of teachers throughout North America. Duncan is the head of the English and Media Arts Department at the School of Experiential Education in Etobicoke, Ontario.

Mariam Khan Durrani was born in Pakistan in 1977 and came to Toronto, Ontario, in 1986. She has been writing poetry and prose since she was seven. "Can't You See?" is taken from her collection of poetry, *Not to Understand*.

Clyde H. Farnsworth was born in 1931 and educated at Yale. He became a reporter in 1954, working for the *New York Herald Tribune* and United Press International before becoming a foreign correspondent for the *New York Times* newspaper in 1963. He has published two books, *No Money Down*, about the American credit industry, and *Out Of This Nettle: A History of Postwar Europe*.

Robert Frost was born in San Francisco, California, in 1874 and grew up in Lawrence, Massachusetts, where he first decided to become a poet. He had his first poem accepted by the *New York Independent* two years after he finished high school. He spent three years in England where he published two books and then returned to the United States to great acclaim and became the unofficial poet laureate. Frost won a Pulitzer Prize in 1923 for his collection *New Hampshire* from which the poem "Stopping by Woods on a

Snowy Evening" is taken. Throughout his life, he maintained that a poem is "never a put-up job... It begins as a lump in the throat, a sense of wrong, a homesickness, a loneliness." He died in Boston, Massachusetts, in 1963.

Natalie Goldberg was born and raised in New York. She decided to become a writer after reading a poem about cooking an eggplant. Up until that time she didn't realize that people could write about ordinary things. She started by writing about her family. Since then she has led writing workshops for high school dropouts, nuns, and senior citizens in New Mexico and Minnesota. She has also written *Writing Down the Bones: Freeing the Writer Within* (from which "Living Twice" is taken) and a collection of poems called *Chicken and in Love*. She lives in Taos, New Mexico.

Kathryn Greenaway was born in Redvers, Saskatchewan, in 1955 and grew up in nearby Saskatoon. She danced professionally for 12 years with the Ballet de Montreal Eddy Toussaint. Then she studied at Concordia University in Montreal and became a journalist. She wrote "Dancers Are Athletes of the Arts World" for *The Gazette* newspaper in Montreal.

Tinker Hatfield, who wrote "Inspired Design: How Nike Puts Emotion in Its Shoes," is Nike's creative director.

Arthur Hoppe was born in 1925 in Honolulu, Hawaii. After studying at Harvard University, he became a reporter and columnist for the *San Francisco Chronicle* in 1949. He is known for his humorous writing—*The Perfect Solution to Absolutely Everything, The Love Everybody Crusade*, and *Dreamboat*.

Langston Hughes was born in 1902 in Joplin, Missouri. His father studied law but was not allowed to take the bar examination because he was black. His mother, who had been a domestic labourer, went on to study at the University of Kansas. Hughes worked as an English teacher in Mexico, a cabin boy on a freighter, a beachcomber, and a launderer before turning to writing full time in 1921. He became well-known for his poetry, plays, essays, stories, and song lyrics, and won many awards. He taught writing at several American universities. Hughes died in New York City in 1967.

Monica Hughes was born in 1925 in Liverpool, England, and lived for a time in Egypt and Rhodesia (now Zimbabwe) before settling in Canada. She became interested in science fiction through her parents' interest in astronomy and by reading the works of Jules Verne. She decided to tackle writing professionally by writing four hours each weekday for a year. Her first book, *Gold-Fever Trail*, was published in 1974 and was soon followed by a number of science fiction novels, including *Crisis on Conshelf Ten* and *Earthdark*. She lives in Edmonton, Alberta.

Evan Hunter was born in 1926 in New York City and lived in an area known as "Italian Harlem" for the first 12 years of his life. He worked at a number of jobs such as selling lobsters and answering telephones before turning to writing full-time. The publisher of his first novel, *The Blackboard Jungle*, suggested he not use his family name of Lombino but his pen name Evan Hunter because it would then sell more copies. He later published a series of mystery novels under the name of Ed McBain. He also wrote plays and screen-plays—Alfred Hitchcock's *The Birds* is one of his most famous—while mainly being recognized as someone who writes about young people. He divides his time between Norwalk, Connecticut, and Sarasota, Florida.

Rita Joe, a Micmac, was born in 1932 in Whycocomagh, Nova Scotia, and grew up in foster families. She entered the Indian Residential School in Shubenacadie at the age of 12. After winning a writing competition in 1974, her response was: "Now my people will think, if she can do it, so can I." Her first book of poems was published in 1978, *Poems of Rita Joe*, and a second collection in 1988, *Song of Eskasoni: More Poems of Rita Joe*, from which "I Lost My Talk" is taken. She lives on the Eskasoni Reserve in Cape Breton and is active in the education of Native children within her family and throughout the country.

Frank Jones was born in Bedfordshire, England, and has lived in Canada for many years. He is a well-known journalist and colum-nist, first for *The Winnipeg Tribune* and then with *The Toronto Star*. His books include a number of analyses of murderers: *Trail of Blood* and *Beyond Suspicion*.

Deborah Kent, who was born in 1948 in Little Falls, New Jersey, has been blind all her life. She was interested in writing throughout school but decided to pursue something more practical so she earned a master's degree in social work at Smith College. A summer vacation to San Miguel de Allende, Mexico, caused her to turn to full-time writing. She wrote her first young-adult novel, *Belonging*, in Mexico. Since then she has written many more novels, including *Cindy* and *That Special Summer*. She lives in Chicago, Illinois.

M. E. Kerr is one of the pen names of Marijane Meaker who was born in Auburn, New York, in 1927. Both of her parents encouraged her love of reading and writing. After attending the University of Missouri, she moved to New York City where she wrote unsuccessful material under a variety of pen names and was fired from a number of jobs because she was more interested in writing than in doing what she was hired to do. Her first story was published in the *Ladies' Home Journal* in 1951 and her first novel, *Spring Fire*, in 1952. She became successful with mysteries and thrillers that she wrote under the names of Vin Packer and Ann Aldrich. In 1964, she published her first young-adult novel. She lives in East Hampton on Long Island, New York.

Keith Leckie is a television writer and director who has written a number of screenplays. He won several awards for "Words on a Page," including a Blue Ribbon in the New York Film Festival.

Janesse Leung is taking theatre and philosophy at McGill University in Montreal, Quebec. She says she believes that "Canadians of Asian or part-Asian descent (like me) should make ourselves heard. We have a unique perspective on Canada, and we can make it known to other Canadians through our stories, plays, poems, and songs." "On a Very Gray Day" appeared in the collection *Asian Voices: Stories From Canada, Korea, China, Vietnam and Japan*. Her home is in Grand Pre, Nova Scotia, where she lives on a small farm.

Bill Majeski was born in 1927 in Meriden, Connecticut. He began his career as a reporter for the *Annapolis Evening Capital* in Maryland and went on to work with the *Washington Daily News* and as a writer of the *Tonight Show*. Since then he has been devoting himself to a career as a free-lance writer, publishing a variety of plays, including *Gross Encounters of the Worst Kind* and *The Maniac Who Came to Dinner*. He lives in Norwalk, Connecticut.

Jean McCallion lives in Hamilton, Ontario, and is a graduate of McMaster University. She published her first collection of poetry, *Apple Love*, in 1981. Her second collection, *Tough Roots*, from which "Tough Roots" is taken, was inspired by her discovery of her Welsh great-grandparents' graves in the Lake Rosseau area, where they settled in 1868. The collection is the story of their homesteading deeds of felling trees, burning slash, uprooting stumps, and building homes and roads.

Andrea Mozarowski was born in Toronto, Ontario, and attended the University of Toronto and Queen's University in Kingston, Ontario. After teaching in Hamilton for several years, she became an English teacher at Upper Canada College, a private school in Toronto. She is interested in studying and teaching about the mass media, particularly in the area of gender representation.

Alden Nowlan was born in 1933 near Windsor, Nova Scotia, and died in 1983 in Fredericton, New Brunswick. He claimed to hold the Canadian record for truancy, "having left school forever after 37 days in Grade 5." At the age of 11 he began writing. He also worked as an unskilled labourer at several temporary jobs. In 1952, he became the news editor of the *Hartland Observer* and began to submit poems to small magazines. He became the writer-in-residence at the University of New Brunswick in 1968 and continued until his death. His poetry collections include *Under the Ice* and *Bread, Wine and Salt*, which won the Governor General's Award in 1967. "Johnnie's Poem" is taken from *Between Tears and Laughter*. Other works include a volume of local history called *Campobello: The Outer Island* and *Double Exposure*, a collection of essays.

Dan Piraro is a cartoonist who has written two books—*Bizarro* and *Post-Modern Bizarro*—in addition to having his cartoons published daily in a number of newspapers. He writes creative biographies of himself, including details about being born "in a remote village off the coast of Missouri" and being a "happy but senseless

257

child." He admits to spending time at an unspecified midwestern university before becoming "Minister of Punctuation" for the state of Louisiana. He says he has little time for cartooning but "continues his daily feature in an effort not to hurt anyone's feelings."

Naomi C. Powell was a Grade 12 student when she wrote the selection "Being Comfortable With Being 'Weird.'" She lives in Campbellville, Ontario.

Winfield Townley Scott was born in 1910 in Haverhill, Massachusetts and died in Santa Fe, New Mexico, in 1968. After studying at Brown University, he became literary editor of the *Providence Journal* and later a full-time poet. His goal was "not to make something beautiful but something true—which in time will be beautiful." His collections of poetry include *To Marry Strangers, The Dark Sister,* and *Scrimshaw.*

Misty Stands in Timber is a Northern Cheyenne student in Lame Deer, Montana. She wrote "As I Walk Along the Hillside" while she was taking a creative writing class in Grade 6. It was published in the 1987–1988 Lame Deer School Poetry Calendar.

Gary Soto is of Mexican descent and was raised in Fresno, California. Although he admits he was no good at school, he went on to study at Fresno City College and California State University. He is a poet, essayist, and young-adult writer with a number of published books: *Black Hair* (from which "Oranges" was taken), *A Fire in My Hands,* and *Living Up the Street.* He teaches in the departments of Chicano Studies and English at the University of California at Berkeley.

Randy Starkman has written articles for newspapers throughout Canada, the United States, and Great Britain. He has travelled in Europe, Australia, and Japan on assignments as a free-lance journalist. His book, *On the Edge,* is about the Canadian women's ski team. He lives in Toronto, Ontario.

Todd Strasser was born in New York City in 1950 and grew up on Long Island. He became a reporter, advertising copywriter, and fiction writer in spite of being "a terrible speller and not a very good writer in high school." He admits he became a writer through the process of elimination after trying medicine and law. His novels for young adults include *Angel Dust Blues, Rock 'n' Roll Nights,* and *A Very Touchy Subject.* He lives in New York City and manages a fortune cookie company, writing what he calls "one-line manuscripts wrapped in cookie dough."

David Suzuki was born in Vancouver, British Columbia, in 1936. A third-generation Japanese-Canadian, he spent his early childhood in a war-time internment camp. He received his Ph.D. from the University of Chicago in Illinois and became a professor at the University of British Columbia in 1969. Internationally known for his work in genetics, Suzuki is dedicated to making science more accessible to non-scientists. As the host of various radio and television shows, including *The Nature of Things,* he explains advances in science and technology in simple terms.

Judith Thompson was born in 1954 in Montreal, and grew up in Connecticut and Ontario. She attended Queen's University in Kingston and the National Theatre School. Since graduating, she has become a successful playwright, winning numerous awards. Her first play was *The Crackwalker,* published in 1980. *White Biting Dog* won the Governor General's Award for drama in 1985. *I Am Yours* won two Dora Awards for acting and a Chalmer's Award in 1987. Her CBC film *Turning to Stone* has been shown throughout the world. She lives in Toronto, Ontario.

Richard Wagamese, who wrote "Shinny Game Melted the Ice" for *Windspeaker,* published by the Aboriginal Multi-Media Society of Alberta, is a regular columnist with that publication. He is also a columnist for the *Calgary Herald* newspaper. His first novel, *Keeper 'N Me,* was published in 1994.

Ed Young was born in 1931 in Tientsin, China, and later moved to the United States. He attended the University of Illinois and Los Angeles Art Center College of Design. Working as an illustrator and designer for many years, he has created drawings for many children's books and folk tales. "Take Time for 8 Matters of the Heart" was part of an illustrated lecture he delivered upon receiving the 1990 Boston Globe-Horn Book Award for *Lon Po Po: A Red-Riding Hood Story From China*. He lives in New York City.

Ian Young was born in London, England, in 1945 and lived for a time in South Africa before making his home in Toronto, Ontario. After studying at the University of Toronto, he edited several small magazines and published a number of collections of poetry: *Year of the Quiet Sun* (from which "Fear of the Landscape" is taken), *Double Exposure*, and *Some Green Moths*.

ACKNOWLEDGEMENTS

Every reasonable effort has been made to acquire permission for copyright material used in this book, and to acknowledge all such indebtedness accurately. However, all errors and omissions called to our attention will be corrected in future printings. In particular, we would be grateful for any information regarding the copyright holders of the following selections: *Fear of the Landscape* by Ian Young and *As I Walk Along the Hillside* by Misty Stands in Timber.

Oranges: From NEW AND SELECTED POEMS by Gary Soto. Copyright © 1995 by Gary Soto. Reprinted by permission of Chronicle Books. *I Loved My Friend*: From THE DREAM KEEPER AND OTHER POEMS by Langston Hughes. Copyright © 1932 by Alfred A. Knopf Inc. and renewed 1960 by Langston Hughes. Reprinted by permission of Alfred A. Knopf, Inc. *Dave's Fall*: by Andrea Holtslander. First appeared in THEMES ON THE JOURNEY (Nelson Canada, 1989). Reprinted by permission of the poet. *Dying for Love*: From PARADISE CAFE AND OTHER STORIES by Martha Brooks (Thistledown Press, 1988). Reprinted by permission of Thistledown Press. *Meg's First Day*: From BELONGING by Deborah Kent. Reprinted by permission of Dial Books for Young Readers, a division of Penguin Books USA Inc. *On the Bridge*: by Todd Strasser. Copyright © 1987 by Todd Strasser. From VISIONS by Donald R. Gallo. Reprinted by permission of Dell Books, a division of Bantam Doubleday Dell Publishing Group, Inc. *Shinny Game Melted the Ice*: by Richard Wagamese. From "Windspeaker", Oct. 25, 1991. Reprinted by permission. *I Lost My Talk*: From SONG OF ESKASONI by Rita Joe. Copyright © by Rita Joe. Reprinted by permission of the author and Ragweed Press. *My Mother*: From MEMORIES HAVE TONGUE by Afua Cooper. Reprinted by permission of Sister Vision Press. *I Am Yours*: From OTHER SIDE OF THE DARK by Judith Thompson. Copyright © 1989 by Judith Thompson. Reprinted by permission of Coach House Press. *Words on a Page*: by Keith Ross Leckie. Based on a story by Daniel David Moses. Reprinted by permission. *Being Comfortable With Being "Weird"*: by Naomi C. Powell. From "The Globe & Mail", June 14, 1993. Reprinted by permission of the author. *Can't You See?*: by Mariam Khan Durrani. Originally appeared in DIVA, June/Aug. 1989. Reprinted by permission of the poet. *Ready, Willing and Able*: by Randy Starkman. From "The Toronto Star", May 1, 1993. Reprinted by permission of the Toronto Star Syndicate. *Take Time for 8 Matters of the Heart*: by Ed Young. From "The Horn Book Magazine", Jan/Feb. 1991. Reprinted by permission of The Horn Book, Inc. *No Place for Teenagers*: by Maria Bohuslawsky. Reprinted by permission of The Ottawa Citizen. *The Essential Mallmanac*: by Phil Patton. From SEVENTEEN Magazine, Aug. 1987. Reprinted by permission of the author. *On the Sidewalk, Bleeding*: From HAPPY NEW YEAR, HERBIE by Evan Hunter. Copyright © 1963 by Hui Corporation. Reprinted by permission of Hui Corporation. *Those Who Don't*: From THE HOUSE ON MANGO STREET by Sandra Cisneros. Copyright © 1984 by Sandra Cisneros. Published by Alfred A. Knopf in 1994 and by Vintage Books, a division of Random House, Inc. in 1991. Reprinted by permission. *A Tanned Version*: by Hummarah Quddoos. From TRUE TO LIFE: WRITINGS BY YOUNG WOMEN edited by Susan Hemmings. Reprinted by permission. *On A Very Gray Day*: by Janesse Leung. Originally appeared in ASIAN VOICES compiled by Terry Watada. Reprinted by permission of the author. *Capturing the Majesty of Nature*: by Tyrone Cashman. Originally appeared as "How We Connect," from *Media&Values* magazine, Fall 1992. Reprinted by permission of Center for Media Literacy, Los Angeles, CA. *Tough Roots*: From TOUGH ROOTS by Jean McCallion. Reprinted by permission of Penumbra Press. *Stopping by Woods on a Snowy Evening*: From THE POETRY OF ROBERT FROST edited by Edward Connery Latham. Copyright © 1951 by Robert Frost. Copyright © 1923, 1969 by Henry Holt & Co., Inc.

Illustrations

Photographs